The First GARCÍA MÁRQUEZ

A Study of His Journalistic Writing From 1948 to 1955

Robert L. Sims

Virginia Commonwealth University

UNIVERSITY
PRESS OF
AMERICA

Lanham • New York • London

Copyright © 1992 by
University Press of America®, Inc.
4720 Boston Way
Lanham, Maryland 20706

3 Henrietta Street
London WC2E 8LU England

Library of Congress Cataloging-in-Publication Data

Sims, Robert Lewis, 1943–
[Primer García Márquez. English]
The first García Márquez : a study of his journalistic writing from
1948 to 1955 / Robert L. Sims.
p.   cm.
Translation of: El primer García Márquez.
Includes bibliographical references and indexes.
1. García Márquez, Gabriel, 1928–   —Criticism
and interpretation.   2. García Márquez, Gabriel,
1928–   —Knowledge—Journalism.   I. Title.
PQ8180.17.A73Z92913   1992   863—dc20   91–43426 CIP

ISBN 0–8191–8577–9 (cloth : alk. paper)
ISBN 0–8191–8578–7 (paper : alk. paper)

To Anne, Laura, Mercedes and Henry

iii

Acknowledgements

Permission to publish selected passages in English translation from the following works is gratefully appreciated:

Gabriel García Márquez. *Obra periodística, Vols. 1-4.* Copyright 1981, 1982 and 1983 by Editorial Bruguera, Barcelona, Spain and permission granted by the author's literary agency, Agencia Literaria Carmen Balcells, S. A., Diagonal 580, 08021 Barcelona, Spain.

Gérard Genette. *Palimpsestes: La Littérature au Second Degré.* Trans. Channa Newman. Copyright to forthcoming edition in English translation is held by the University Press of Nebraska, Lincoln, Nebraska, which has given me permission to quote certain passages.

Víctor Rodríguez Núñez, "La peregrinación de la jirafa. García Márquez: su periodimso costeño." *Casa de las Américas* 23.137 (March/April, 1983), 27-39.

Pedro Sorela. *El otro García Márquez: Los años difíciles.* Copyright 1988 by Mondadori, Madrid, Spain and permission granted by the author's literary agency, Kerrigan/Miró Literary Agency, Trav. de Gracia 12, 08021 Barcelona, Spain.

Permission also granted by *Chasqui* to publish my article, "La serie de La Sierpe de García Márquez: la política de la narración o cómo narrar la política," XVI.1 (February, 1987), 45-53 as Chapter 6.

Abbreviations and Foreign Word Usage

The following abbreviations will be used in this book: <u>OHYS</u> (<u>One Hundred Years of Solitude</u> and <u>AP</u> (<u>The Autumn of the Patriarch</u>). In all other cases, the full titles of works are given. I have also retained the Spanish words "costeño" and "cachaco" because their English translations are inadequate. "Costeño" means costal, or an inhabitant of the coast, but it also expresses a sociocultural attitude characteristic of the Atlantic coast of Colombia which emerges in García Márquez's work. It connotes openness, vitality, warmth, the sea, and spontaneity, and García Márquez often contrasts this attitude with the cheerless seriousness of the "cachacos," or people from the interior, especially Bogotá. Finally, I have also retained the Spanish word "jirafa" (giraffe) which is the name of the column which García Márquez wrote for the Barranquilla newspaper <u>El Heraldo</u> from 1950 to 1952.

Contents

Introduction

Gabriel García Márquez, Nobel Prize for Literature and Journalism?

On the morning of Thursday, October 21, 1982, the world awoke to the news that the enigmatic Swedish Academy had selected Gabriel García Márquez to receive the Nobel Prize for Literature. Like the universal critical and popular acclaim of his novel *OHYS*, the selection of García Márquez was also greeted with equal enthusiasm. He thus became the fourth Latin American writer to receive the prize, following Gabriela Mistral (1945), Miguel Angel Asturias (1967) and Pablo Neruda (1973). Nowhere was the response more jubilant than in the town of Aracataca, Colombia, where García Márquez was born on March 6, 1928:

> With a temperature of 90 in the shade, the parents of the author of *One Hundred Years of Solitude* headed up a throng of people which wended its way through the streets of the town until they arrived at the house where the author was born, and it was proclaimed a national monument. Before that a small plane had bombarded the whole place with thousands of yellow butterflies and flowers, and a herd of wild horses had been turned loose. Afterwards, Luisa Santiaga and Gabriel Eligio presided over a public banquet during which thirty-three sheep, four hundred chickens, three thousand pieces of fish, four thousand yucca rolls and an undetermined number of bottles of rum were consumed.[1]

This carnivalesque celebration of García Márquez's Nobel Prize not only corresponds very closely to the reality of his fiction but also contrasts sharply with the seriousness of the official world of the Swedish Academy where the prize originates.

In the case of García Márquez, the significance of the Nobel Prize for Literature and the reasons why he was chosen, differ

1

considerably depending on the source. Whether the opinions come from members of the Swedish Academy, general readers of his work, literature students or critics, most would probably emphasize his narrative fiction, single out *OHYS*, talk about his universal vision, or compare his fictional universe to that of William Faulkner, a writer whom García Márquez has deeply admired since 1950. While these explanations are certainly valid, his selection signifies much more than one work, or, for that matter, his entire corpus of prose fiction; rather the Nobel Prize must also include García Márquez's work as a journalist which spans more than forty years starting in 1948. However, many critics, like Stephen Minta, have preferred to attribute only minor importance to this facet of his work: "García Márquez's early journalism, dating from the years 1948 to 1960, has recently been published in four volumes, edited by Jacques Gilard. Little of it would ever be read today, were it not for García Márquez's literary status, and a great deal of it was clearly constrained by the fact that he began his newspaper work as a columnist, not as a reporter."[2] Nevertheless, Minta adds that "the early experience in Cartagena, followed by a period in Barranquilla where, from 1950 to 1952, he wrote for another Liberal newspaper, *El Heraldo*, was of critical importance in determining the future direction of his career."[3]

While Minta's statement about García Márquez's current literary status helps explain the publication of his early journalism, his assertion that little of it would be read today if he were not famous and that its literary value is limited by the fact that he started as a columnist, fails to underscore its crucial importance in the initial phase of García Márquez's writing from 1947 to 1955. As Raymond L. William explains:

> Journalism has been a constant presence in García Márquez's literary and personal biography. García Márquez the novelist has gained far more from journalism than just "contact with reality." There were crucial initial lessons in writing for the general public---and the related fictionalization of the reader. Certain techniques considered basic to journalism have become

constant in García Márquez's fiction: the creation of a high level of interest from the very first lines of a text; the use of journalistic details. The broad range of fictional styles and techniques with which he became acquainted during the early years on the coast undoubtedly afforded new possibilities for his journalism. A reading of his journalistic writings during this period, in fact, shows a writer experimenting with a variety of styles, techniques and genres. Both the enormous volume of García Márquez's journalism and its intimate relationship to his fiction make his journalistic writings essential to a complete study of his work.[4]

García Márquez has been, since the inception of his writing career, primarily a journalist-fiction writer, and the evolution of his work has involved a continuous interaction of the two genres. Victor Rodríguez Núñez clearly delineates the importance of García Márquez's journalism to his writing: "The popular enthusiasm notwithstanding, I agree completely with Jorge Timossi that 'the Nobel Prize for Literature awarded to García Márquez is also especially a Nobel Prize for Journalism,' for his journalism. The thirty-five years dedicated to the systematic practice of his profession which he himself has defined as 'the noblest profession in the world'---materialized in hundreds of commentaries, chronicles, news stories and articles on the widest range of subjects and written with the same precision and brilliance as his best pages of fiction---constitute the most forceful argument in our favor."[5]

Many of the interesting pages to which Rodríguez Núñez refers were written from 1948 to 1955, and it has only been since 1981 with the publication of García Márquez's journalistic writings in four volumes that readers and critics outside Colombia have had more direct access to these texts. While the publication history of García Márquez's work partially accounts for the reduced number of studies of his journalism, there still remains a general tendency to downgrade its importance in relation to his literary work. García

Márquez's own works resist any attempt to classify them as either journalism or fiction, and two of his most recent works, *Chronicle of a Death Foretold* (1981) and *Clandestine in Chile: The Adventures of Miguel Littín* (1986), reaffirm the continuous, intimate relationship between journalism and literature. *Chronicle of a Death Foretold* has generated a heated controversy over its status as a novel or a glorified remake of a news story disguising itself as a novel, and part of the polemic can be attributed to the interplay of journalism and fiction in the work.[6] Apart from the brief periods during which García Márquez only seemed to write fiction, he has essentially remained a journalist-fiction writer, and journalism has never served as just a simple backdrop for his fiction.

Rodríguez Núñez mentions several misleading generalizations which this study also proposes to refute.[7] The first purports that García Márquez's journalistic writing mainly served as an apprenticeship stage in which he learned how to write using different styles. This narrow perspective reduces the enormous volume of his journalistic writing to a collection of exercises in style devoid of any intrinsic literary value. While the development of a style is certainly an important aspect of these texts, it constitutes only one facet which can be studied. A second erroneous idea is to view his journalistic writing, especially the texts written between 1948 and 1955 which represent the primary focus of the present study, as mere pre-texts for his later fiction writing. This perspective assumes that these early texts held no interest for anyone until García Márquez wrote *OHYS* in 1967. However, as Rodríguez Núñez points out, "García Márquez's journalism was of extraordinary interest to readers independent of his first published short stories, long before the appearance of his first novel, and even more than all his fiction writing up to the appearance in 1967---that is, when he was completing the second decade of his passionate devotion to 'the noblest profession in the world'---of *One Hundred Years of Solitude*."[8] García Márquez's journalistic writings from 1948 to 1955 thus not only constitute the first stage of his writing but also represent a major force in his development as a writer.

The first chapter establishes the critical framework for analyzing García Márquez's bigeneric writing. Besides examining the relation between journalism and literature, this chapter presents the critical perspectives which will be employed to analyze the journalistic writing of the Colombian author. These methods include the narrative codes set out by Roland Barthes, narratology, Gérard Genette's concept of transtextuality and the theoretical ideas of the Russian critic Mikhail Bakhtin (his concepts are often labelled dialogic criticism or dialogism). Above all, this chapter provides the global, critical framework in which the subsequent chapters will continue to explore García Márquez's writing as a bigeneric phenomenon.

Chapter 2 focuses on a series of ten texts which García Márquez wrote between 1948 and 1950 when he worked as a columnist for *El Universal* in Cartagena. The application of Genette's transtextuality shows how García Márquez takes advantage of the open format of the column to write on a variety of topics and to include various genres which belong to the literary domain. The transtextual analysis of these columns clearly demonstrates that, even at this early stage, García Márquez is already developing his bigeneric writing. Chapter 3 centers on a series of eighteen pieces which García Márquez wrote as a columnist for *El Heraldo* in Barranquilla between 1950 and 1952. This phase represents a crucial step in the development of his writing, and the nearly four hundred pieces called *jirafas* that he produced, contain many elements that will form the basis of his subsequent writing. While the principal critical focus remains transtextual, its broad scope opens the way for including other methods which will elucidate the relation and interaction between journalism and literature.

Chapter 4 centers on the journalistic work that García Márquez did for the Liberal Bogota newspaper, *El Espectador*, from February, 1954 to July, 1955. During this period he devoted his efforts to three different areas: film criticism, pieces written for the column "Day to Day," and a series of longer articles and feature stories which mark his entry into the field of investigative reporting.

This chapter focuses on three of these longer reportages which not only elucidate the intimate relation between journalism and literature, but also show how each one constitutes another step leading to the direct confrontation with the official world and its power. García Márquez's collision course with the official world will reach critical mass in his long series entitled *The Story of a Shipwrecked Sailor*.

Chapter 5 deals with a fourteen part series on the sailor Luis Alejandro Velasco who was swept overboard when his ship was buffeted by high waves. He spent ten harrowing days adrift in a life raft before reaching the Atlantic coast of Colombia. This series, which first appeared first in April, 1955 in *El Espectador* and then in 1970 in book form with the title *The Story of a Shipwrecked Sailor*, represents a decisive step in the development of García Márquez's narrative techniques, the creation of a double narrator and the involvement of the reader as a transitive participant. This work also delineates the author's dualist position in relation to power. Chapter 6 examines the series that García Márquez wrote on the coastal region called La Sierpe. He interweaves journalistic, political and literary discourses to produce a hybridized text which transcends generic boundaries. The portrayal of the social organization of La Sierpe not only prefigures the early stages of Macondo in *OHYS*, but also reveals how García Márquez communicates his political vision in a narrative form.

This book would have not been possible without the generous support of different people who have contributed in various ways to the completion of this book. First, my sincere gratitude goes to my colleagues and friends in the Association of Colombianists for keeping me in contact with Colombian reality; to Virginia Commonwealth University whose grant enabled me to devote my energies to this project; and last, and in no way least, to my wife, Anne, who initiated me into the mysteries and marvels of the computer, to Buddy LaBrenz, our former departmental secretary, and to Sherry Lane, our senior secretary, who helped me with the manuscript.

Notes

1.   Victor Rodríguez Núñez, "La peregrinación de la jirafa. García Márquez: su periodismo costeño," *Casa de las Américas* 23.137 (March-April, 1983), 27-8. Translations are mine.

2.   Stephen Minta, *García Márquez: Writer of Colombia* (New York: Harper & Row, 1987), 41.

3.   Minta, 4I.

4.   Raymond L. Williams, *Gabriel García Márquez* (Boston: Twayne, 1984), 134.

5.   Rodríguez Núñez, 28.

6.   Carmen Rabell, *Periodismo y ficción en Crónica de una muerte anunciada* (Santiago: Instituto Profesional del Pacífico, 1985), 13-15. She gives a brief summary of the controversy raised by the work in various critical circles.

7.   Rodríguez Núñez, 38-9.

8.   Rodríguez Núñez, 39.

Chapter 1

García Márquez, Journalism, Fiction and the Quest for Bigeneric Writing: The Critical Foundations

The focus of this study could raise the objection that it really concentrates on two distinct and fundamentally dissimilar genres, journalism and literature. Therefore, critics would have to separate García Márquez's journalism from his literary works to avoid superimposing a critical framework which would violate the integrity of each genre. Indeed, despite the enormous quantity and the high quality of García Márquez's journalism, critics have, until recently, concentrated almost exclusively on his fiction, and they have relegated his journalism to a parenthetical, incidental role. This position might be justified if the development of García Márquez's career clearly showed that he has been *successively* a journalist and novelist, and not a journalist-fiction writer. In short, the problem consists of answering the question: Has García Márquez always been and does he continue to be an journalist-fiction writer, or rather, alternately a journalist and fiction writer?

While the question may appear simple, the answer proves to be much more problematical.   The "official" debut of García Márquez's career points to an independent beginning and development of each genre, since his first short stories appeared in 1947 and his first journalistic piece in 1948.[1]   Neither date, however, contributes in any substantial way to the resolution of the problem. While a cursory examination of his writing career reveals that during certain periods one genre tends to dominate the other, this overview does not elucidate the kind of writing which produces a work at a particular stage.   Although the rhythm of García Márquez's production follows a constant but variable pattern, he has nonetheless continued to write in both genres without significant interruptions.   While it may seem more difficult to find an abundance of concrete instances where his fiction and journalism interface, the publication of *Chronicle of a Death Foretold* in 1981 exemplifies the bigeneric nature of his writing. The novel quickly provoked a heated debate about its generic

9

status: "Is *Chronicle of a Death Foretold* a novel of the stature or quality of author's previous works, or is it simply a residual product which can be classified as a type of subliterature or, worse still, an inconsequential journalistic chronicle?"[2]   The intense debate generated by this novel suggests that García Márquez's work consciously endeavors to break down the barriers between genres. While *Chronicle of a Death Foretold* offers clear evidence of García Márquez's bigeneric writing, it does not conclusively resolve the issue.

Another approach is to consider the respective origins of the novel and journalism. Aníbal González states that

> journalism and the modern novel have been interacting with and interpenetrating each other since their respective origins in the seventeenth and eighteenth centuries, and similarities between the institution of journalism and the genre of the novel abound. The modern novel arose with the picaresque and *Don Quijote* in the midst of the Renaissance dilemma of distinguishing history from fiction. Journalism is derived from a textual amalgam that unhierarchically encompasses news items, essays, and narrative prose. From the beginning both genres have shared a similar conception of knowledge and representation: that which was explicitly formulated by English empiricism and which emphasizes the role of the senses, particularly sight, in the acquisition of knowledge. The novel itself is a radically mimetic genre that tends to imitate other genres and subgenres such as the letter, the historical chronicle, legal depositions, and journalistic articles.[3]

Beyond the inevitable academic controversies about the origins of the modern novel and journalism, the similar sociohistorical conditions of their beginnings and their shared patterns of development strongly indicate that they are interactive genres.

Raúl Rivadeneira Prada marks the beginning of modern journalism in 1702: "With the appearance of the first English daily newspaper, the *Daily Courant*, in 1702, a profound change in journalism takes place. The appearance of the *Daily Courant* establishes the concept of the daily publication of information about public events and of general interest. The principle of objectivity also becomes the norm for the transmission of information in the print media."[4] This crucial change in the way of informing the public also relates to the development of a new journalistic discourse based on narrative components. These interactive genres create new channels for narrating/transmitting information and events.

The position of each genre in modern society can also shed light on their interrelationship. The study of language as communication within its social context correlates to metalinguistics, a concept developed by the Russian critic, Mikhail Bakhtin. Tzvetan Todorov defines metalinguistics (or translinguistics in his parlance) as "the discipline that studies the stable, nonindividual, forms of discourse."[5] Bakhtin says that "every particular utterance is assuredly individual, but each sphere of language use develops its own *relatively stable types* of utterances, and that is what we call *discursive genres*."[6] Bakhtin believes that metalinguistics can fully elucidate the history and social life of language, which includes a broad spectrum of oral and written genres. Besides anchoring the text in the matrix of circumstances in which it was written, Bakhtin's focus examines the cultural codes that connect the reader to the text.

Bakhtin specifies two types of speech genres: primary (simple) and secondary (complex) speech genres. The primary speech genres are oral and encompass a seemingly inexhaustible variety of discourses like the short rejoinders of daily dialogue, everyday narration, or dinner conversation. Bakhtin notes that "the wealth and diversity of speech genres are boundless because the various possibilities of human activity are inexhaustible, and because each sphere of activity contains an entire repertoire of speech genres that differentiate and grow as the particular sphere develops and becomes more complex."[7] Secondary (complex) speech genres embrace "novels, dramas, all kinds of scientific research, major genres of commentary, [and they] arise in more complex and comparatively highly developed and organized cultural communication (primarily written) that is artistic, scientific, sociopolitical, and so on."[8] These two speech genres are closely allied because the secondary speech genres continuously "absorb and digest various primary (simple) genres that have taken form in unmediated speech communion."[9]

Since we live in a chirographic society (with writing), the idea of a society based on orality constitutes, although mistakenly, a "primitive" stage in human evolution.[10] This negative view of orality does not mean that it has lost its importance in modern society; rather primary orality has changed into what Walter J. Ong has perceptively called "secondary orality": "This new orality has striking resemblances to the old in its participatory mystique, its fostering of a communal sense, its concentration on the present moment, and even its use of formulas. But it is essentially a more deliberate and self-conscious orality, based permanently on the use of writing and print."[11] We thus live in a society in which the mass media profoundly and undeniably influence all aspects of our lives.

Despite the constant interaction of the two genres in modern society, the novel has attained a much higher status than journalism: "The literary upper class were the novelists. They were regarded as the only 'creative' writers, the only literary artists. The middle class were the 'men of letters,' the literary essayists, the more authoritative critics. The lower class were the journalists, and they were so low down in the structure that they were barely noticed at all."[12] This classification system denies the reality of the intergeneric development of the novel and journalism: "The fact that both journalism and the novel are of 'low' rhetorical origins and are notoriously lacking poetics, is another sign of their common modernity; the novel's 'journalism' emphasizes 'novelty,' the newness of its stories and of itself as a genre".[13] Although both genres have resisted persistent attempts to define them, they have spawned many subgenres like the historical novel, the psychological novel, the romantic, the realistic and naturalist novel and interpretive, electronic and investigative journalism. These subgenres, instead of contributing to global definitions of the novel and journalism, reaffirm their vitality, diversity and definitional resistance.

We can now at least rephrase our initial question: What is the most productive method to study the journalistic-literary work of García Márquez? Aníbal González suggests a bigeneric approach: "If it is impossible to distinguish journalism from literature by appealing to absolute formal or stylistic criteria, what are we to do with the huge mass of journalistic texts produced by an author like García Márquez?"[14] After considering several possible methods, he proposes exploring "those instances in which journalism is explicitly alluded to, thematized, parodied, or otherwise self-consciously placed in the foreground of the literary text."[15] Within this framework, narrative discourse emerges as one of the most solid links between journalism and the novel. Tom Wolfe also emphasizes the importance of narrative discourse in his discussion of new journalism: "It showed me the possibility of there being something 'new' in journalism. What interested me was not simply the discovery that it was possible to write accurate non-fiction with techniques usually associated with novels and short stories. It was that---plus. It was the discovery that it was possible in non-fiction, in journalism, to use any literary device, from the traditional dialogisms of the essay to stream-of-consciousness, and to use many different kinds simultaneously, or within a relatively short space to excite the reader both intellectually and emotionally."[16]

Wolfe delineates the problem of the journalist in relation to the space of print journalism which is governed by a much more formal and restrictive set of rules than the space of the novel. In general, the journalist writes under pressure because he has deadlines to meet. Frequently, his topic does not extend beyond the immediate reality of that day's edition, and his article must conform to strict space requirements imposed by the newspaper. The journalist must constantly deal with a panoply of spatio-temporal limitations which have become formal elements of journalism's generic makeup.   According to Wolfe, narrative discourse offers the journalist the only realistic measure of freedom in the face of such stringent conventions. Bakhtin underscores the limitations placed on the journalist who "is above all a contemporary. He is obliged to be one. He lives in the sphere of questions that can be resolved in the present day (or in any case in the near future). He participates in a dialogue that can be ended and even finalized, can be translated into action, and can become an empirical force. It is precisely in this sphere that 'one's own word' is possible. Outside this sphere 'one's own word' is not one's own (the individual personality always transcends itself); 'one's own word' cannot be the ultimate word."[17] Since the novel and journalism lack global definitions that prevent their generic intersection, and they exhibit a great capacity for adapting to changing environments, these genres will inevitably clash with the centripetal forces of artificial conventions. Even though the horizons of the novel seem much broader than those of journalism, the journalist must introduce his word into the inconclusive and infinite dialogue to find other ways to achieve his goal.

Wolfe believes that the journalist discovers this freedom in the techniques of the novel. They not only enable him to extend the reach of his word beyond the confines of journalistic space but also to surmount the conventions *within* the same limitations. If the journalist seeks to overcome the formal limits of journalism by using literary methods, the novelist often draws on journalism to create his fictional reality. From a historical standpoint, Wolfe focuses on the connection between the two genres which culminated in the realistic novel of the 19th century. The realistic novel, seemingly abandoned by modern literature, was rediscovered by the American new journalists in the 1970s: "By trial and error, by 'instinct' rather than theory, journalists began to discover the devices that gave the realistic novel its unique power, variously known as its 'immediacy,' its 'concrete reality,' its 'emotional involvement,' its 'gripping' or 'absorbing' quality."[18]

Wolfe enumerates four techniques that the new journalists rediscovered: scene-by-scene construction, realistic dialogue, the third person point of view and the detailed recording of the material aspects of existence.[19] From the viewpoint of modern literary criticism, this "discovery" does not seem very remarkable, especially in view of the rapid, exponential development of new perspectives in the last twenty years. On the contrary, new journalism seemed determined to revert to a past literary tradition that the modern novel had already surpassed and discarded a long time ago. This would be true if we disregarded the twin births and interfacial evolution of the two genres and, perhaps more important, their great flexibility and adaptability to swift sociocultural changes. The union of new journalism and the realistic novel represents a logical outcome since both genres employ narrative discourse and techniques to transmit a common vision of reality. Returning to the past to find this historical intersection also reaffirms the continuous interaction and the coequal status of the two genres, but this does not mean that either Wolfe, the new journalist, or García Márquez, is going to adhere completely to the techniques of the realistic novel. Above all, Wolfe endeavors to anchor new journalism in a literary tradition.

These two bastard genres have continued to grow and diversify until, today, they are by far the most widely disseminated, written, heard and seen secondary speech genres because their ability to change and adapt enables them to reach large audiences by addressing the different senses. Within the proliferating forms of mass media we find electronic and televised journalism, the cine-novel and the cassette-novel. Ultimately, it does not much matter that in many critical circles the novel is considered a "serious literary genre," and journalism a "popular" genre, a kind of paraliterature not worthy of serious study, because journalism and the novel simply continue to interact. Journalism does possess literary qualities and many novels freely borrow from journalism.

Whatever label we use, the journalistic novel, non-fiction literature or the literature of fact, the analysis of a journalist-fiction writer like García Márquez can base itself on modern critical methods to establish the vital interrelation of both genres without reducing them to an inventory of techniques. In this continuous generic interaction, each one hybridizes the other so that the journalistic and novelistic utterances can occupy new contexts. Narrative discourse constitutes the most viable link between journalism and the novel, and it lies at the center of the study of the interrelation of the two genres.

Within the present critical panorama, despite the proliferation of new perspectives and the concomitant terminological pro(con)fusion, the one constant is the *text*, the object on which the conflicting voices of critical discourse center. While no single critical method can claim to act as a "pilot science" for the study of literature, narrativity links all these perspectives. As Gérard Genette explains, "the vast majority of literary (including poetic) texts are in the narrative mode and it is therefore proper for narrativity to appropriate to itself the lion's share."[20] Genette adds that, although the narrative text can be studied from other angles, "the best, or the worst---in any case, the strongest--- justification for the momentary hegemony of narratology seems to me to derive not so much from the importance of the object as from narratology's own degree of maturation and methodological elaboration."[21] The term *narratology*, proposed by Tzvetan Todorov in 1969, has various definitions. Narratology "studies the nature, form, and functioning of narrative (regardless of medium of representation) and tries to characterize narrative competence."[22] It also "examines what all and only narratives have in common (at the level of story, narrating, and their relations) as well as what enables them to be different from one another, and it attempts to account for the ability to produce and understand them."[23] From a more restricted point of view, narratology studies "narration as a verbal mode of representation of temporally ordered situations and events."[24] This narratological perspective disregards the story level in itself and focuses on the possible relations between the story and the narrative discourse.

Narratology has sometimes been criticized for its excessive technicality and its mechanical application to the study of texts, but as Genette aptly observes, "the mechanics of narratology---a mechanics that, I think, has nothing of a general philosophy about it but that at its best is distinguished by a *respect for the mechanisms of the text*."[25] Instead of producing a mechanical study of the text, the textual perspective reveals the gross constituents (that is, the codes and the textual relations) on which the narrativity of the text bases itself. While no single perspective can exhaust the possibilities of the text, a group of related methods can show how the macroelements of narrativity combine to produce the magic of what we call the text. Narrativity transcends generic boundaries because all texts narrate something. Moreover, when the analysis focuses on the work of a writer like García Márquez, whose corpus includes a large quantity of journalistic and literary texts, the textual focus (which includes narratology, codes and transtextuality) enables us to view his work as a bigeneric production.

Besides narratology, the approach of Roland Barthes focuses on textual codes. To decodify a text, Barthes proposes breaking up the text in a completely arbitrary manner and dividing it into *lexias*, or reading units. Each unit reveals certain codes that pass through the text, so that at any and all points we can detect the different intersections of the codes. Barthes identifies five textual codes:

1) the *proairetic* code, which provides the basis of events and sequences, proliferating linearly and irreversibly;

2) the *semic* code, which provides the basis of character traits;

3) the *hermeneutic* code, which provides the basis of a macrostructure linearly and irreversibly directed towards closure;

4) the *symbolic* code, which provides the basis of representation through reversible binary oppositions;

5) the *reference* code, which provides the basis of seemingly extra-textual referentiality.[26]

The proairetic code "gives a narrative its potential to organize a story as a linear sequencing of events occurring in time."[27] The semic code "inscribes the field where signifiers point to other signifiers to produce the chain of recognizable connotations."[28] The hermeneutic code "is the code of narrative suspense [and] raises the basic question: what will happen next in the story and why?"[29] The symbolic code is the most complex and "marks out the textual zone of representation" and, as its name indicates, "one sign stands in for---and so represents---another."[30] The referential code is composed of "references to a science or a body of knowledge; in drawing attention to them, we merely indicate the type of knowledge (physical, physiological, medical, psychological, literary, historical, etc.) referred to, without going so far as to construct (or reconstruct) the culture they express."[31] For this reason, this code "is thus a general category of the many culture codes which speak through us and to us whenever we use language."[32] Barthes adds an important proviso concerning the codes: "The five codes create a kind of network, a *topos* through which the entire text passes (or rather, in passing, becomes text). Thus, if we make no effort to structure each code, or the five codes among themselves, we do so deliberately, in order to assume the multivalence of the text, its partial reversibility. We are, in fact, concerned not to manifest a structure but to produce a structuration".[33] The fifth code, by addressing a wider context, leads to the concept of transtextuality proposed by Gérard Genette.

Genette defines transtextuality as the "textual transcendence of the text," that is, "the group of general, or transcendent, categories---types of discourse, modes of utterance, literary genres, etc.---from which each text arises."[34] Within transtextuality Genette distinguishes fives types of transtextual relations:

intertextuality, paratextuality, metatextuality, hypertextuality and architextuality. Intertextuality is characterized by "a relation of copresence between two or more texts; that is, eidetically or most frequently, by the actual presence of one text in another."[35] Another form of intertextuality that Genette does not mention is "the existence, alongside *general* intertextuality and *restricted* intertextuality, of an *autarchic* intertextuality."[36] This autarchic intertextuality is called *autotextuality* and an *autotext* is defined as "an internal reduplication that doubles the narrative *completely or partially in its literal form* (strictly speaking, that of the *story*) or *referentially* (the form of the *fiction*)."[37]

Paratextuality is constituted by "the generally less explicit and more distant relationship which---within the whole that makes up a literary text---the text proper maintains with what can only be called a paratext: title, subtitle, explanatory notes, afterwards, introductions, etc."[38] Metatextuality "is the relation, what is commonly called 'commentary,' that links one text to another, of which it speaks without necessarily citing it (calling it forth), or even, in the most extreme case, without naming it."[39] The fourth type of transtextuality is hypertextuality, which Genette defines as "every relationship that joins a text B (which I will call the *hypertext*) to a previous text A (which, of course, I will call the *hypotext*) on which it is grafted in a manner which is not that of commentary."[40] Genette offers the following example of hypertextuality: "*The Eneid* and *Ulysses* are undoubtedly, in different degrees and certainly with different titles, two (among others) hypertexts of a same hypotext: *The Odyssey*, of course. If *The Eneid* and *Ulysses* share the common trait of not deriving from *The Odyssey* like some page of *The Poetics* derives from *Oedipus Rex*, that is, by commenting on it, but by a transformational operation, these two works stand out among them, considering that in the case of these two works the same type of transformation is not involved. The transformation which leads from *The Odyssey* to *Ulysses* can be described as a *simple*, or *direct* transformation: that which consists of transferring the action of the *Odyssey* to the Dublin of the twentieth century."[41]

Architextuality "involves a completely silent relation which at best, only a paratextual mention articulates, and of a purely taxonomic nature."[42] In other words, in architextuality the relation is more implicit because it depends on the combination of all the factors which contribute to the form of a particular text.

Although the above discussion presents a general theoretical picture of textual analysis, the combination of these different perspectives---narratology, Bakhtinian metalinguistics, Barthes's textual codes and Genette's transtextuality---furnishes a multiple, analytical approach which enables us to study literary and journalistic texts in a more integrated and global manner. Narratology and textual codes show how narrative discourse functions within the textual boundaries. The fifth textual code proposed by Barthes extends the reach of narrative discourse beyond the text to include the extratextual dimension, so that the text can link up with all the codes which are anchored in the language we use and in the texts we read. The transtextual components establish the relations of every text with other texts, whether they involve internal or external relations. As Genette says, "there exist no texts without textual transcendence."[43] Transtextuality redefines and amplifies the concept of intertextuality first formulated by Julia Kristeva, thus creating an extensive network of possible relations.

These critical methods overcome the artificial generic conventions which only obscure the textual and transtextual reality that links journalism and the novel. To examine García Márquez's fiction and journalism separately and according to a set of fixed criteria amounts to falsifying his work, to classifying it according to the same norms which his works constantly contradict and undermine. This is not to suggest that García Márquez only writes to subvert the generic conventions; more often he writes within them, but through narrative discourse and the constant interaction of both genres, he produces works which dissolve the artificial barriers and establish a dialogic framework in which the genres merge and diverge in continuous fashion. The evolution of García

Márquez's bigeneric work does not consist of leaving journalistic or literary "footprints": rather his work springs from the *interactive process* of two genres which was set in motion with his first journalistic piece in 1948. If García Márquez's writing is a process, it implies a certain unfinalization that derives from the same generic interaction.

The critical framework for studying the bigeneric work of García Márquez would remain incomplete without situating him in relation to each genre. Raúl Rivadeneira Prada's definition of print journalism provides a point of departure: "It is an open system of human, technologized communication which processes events, ideas and feelings coming from one or various sources in order to transmit them to a receptor through a journalistic channel."[44] To this definition we must add the basic elements which open communication systems have in common:

Message---Code---Communicator or Codifier---Medium---Receiver or Decodifier[45]

If these are the elements of the system, the transmission the information follows a slightly different path:

Source---Codifier---Message---Decodifier---Receiver[46]

According to Rivadeneira Prada, the source is the "reason that generates the piece of news and represents the stimulus for the codifier in his communication intention."[47] The communicator or codifier "is the element which has the task of translating the signs and signals from the source, that is, the journalist, chronicler, reporter, editor, editorialist, etc.[48] The message "is the communicable product which, composed of signs/signals emanating from an event, the codifier produces."[49] The decodifier "is the agent in opposition to the codifier; it signifies the element which selects (deciphers) the printed message-news item, and also in a psychointellectual process which takes place in the receiver."[50] The decodifier also designates the "agent who perceives the decodified message" [and] "who reacts to the message, thus producing a characteristic phenomenon of mass communication known as *feedback*."[51]

These elements allow us to define the respective roles of the novelist and journalist. While the journalist receives his information from a variety of sources, he must remain within the framework of the source.[52]   Often the journalist has to investigate, gather information and become an instant expert on a subject to be able to write his article and, in principle, he cannot improvise or embellish his material.   Unlike the journalist, the novelist has nothing to "know," because he invents everything.   Certainly, a novel can also be based on a historical event, or a news story, like *Chronicle of a Death Foretold*, but the event normally serves as a starting point for the novelist.   The novelist can also amass documentation about an event, but from that point on, he invents the story.   Therefore, the most important aspect is *how the story is narrated* (narrative discourse relates more closely to the hermeneutic code and *writerly* literature in which the reader is a transitive participant), and not *what happened* (the narrated segment is more closely affiliated with the linear sequencing of the proairetic code that Barthes links to *readerly* literature in which the reader is an intransitive participant).

The differences between the journalist and the novelist with respect to narrative discourse turn out to be more apparent than real.   According to Barthes, the *fait-divers* (often referred to as a filler in journalism, a short item used in a publication to fill space, generally at the bottom of a column) violates our notions of causality, and coincidence and chance play an important role.[53] The *fait-divers* is the most "literary" form of the news because the inverse causality, coincidences and irony which this type of journalism uses (it is called reportorial journalism which is characterized by an objective, factual writing style, rather than subjective, interpretive criticism or commentary), resemble the narrative strategies employed by the novelist.[54]   Like many forms of literature, the news story tends to be imminent; that is, "all" of the necessary facts are presented to the reader to cause a certain effect (surprise, laughter, horror, sadness, etc.). As in literature, the news story exists in a twilight zone in which causality and chance compete for domination, and interpretation can never reach a finalized and complete explanation. Barthes adds that "all these paradoxes of causality have a double meaning; on the one hand, the notion of causality is reinforced by them, since we feel that the cause is everywhere: here the *fait-divers* tells us that man is always linked to something else, that nature is full of echoes, relations, and movements; but on the other hand, this same causality is constantly undermined by forces which escape it."[55] The ostensibly closed system of causality is constantly penetrated by chance and coincidence, or elements which in narratology correspond to *anachronies*: "Narration is a doubly temporal sequence, the time of the narrated and the time of narration (the time of signified and the time of the signifier)."[56] These anachronies can be *analepses* (an evocation of one or more events that occurred before the "present" moment, or moment when the chronological recounting of a sequence of events is interrupted to make room for the analepsis), or a *prolepsis* (an evocation of one or more events that will occur after the "present" moment, or moment when the chronological recounting of a sequence of events is interrupted to make room for the prolepsis).[57]

Barthes's analysis of the news story opens the way for the critical perspectives which we have been developing and stresses the important role that narrative discourse plays in both genres. Since García Márquez starts his career working in two genres whose spatial configurations and formal criteria appear to separate them, the principal link between them does not reside in the narrated but in narrative discourse. García Márquez's writing never seeks to displace one genre in favor of the other; that is, there is no overt rivalry in which domination is the goal. As we have repeatedly stated, García Márquez's writing is an *interactive process* whose basis is narrative discourse and whose major characteristic is the exploration of the textual links between the two genres. If García Márquez never endeavors to separate or transcend a genre, if he attributes equal weight to each one, and given the dynamic evolution of his writing, his works are products of an intimate, synergetic and dialogical association to which journalism and literature contribute in a continuous fashion.

In literature (especially the detective novel) and journalism, one of the most often used events is a murder. Although the journalist and the novelist can use the same narrative form (that is, starting at the end and reconstructing the facts leading up to the crime), the novelist appears to enjoy more narrative freedom because he invents everything and can order the events without adhering to a strict chronology. This technique is called a broken line narrative: "In this type of narration the author plays with time on different levels, in a kind of counterpoint between the present and the past. The past does not necessarily appear at one moment but possibly at several points. As a general rule, the narration begins in the present, then returns to various moments in the past, and circles back to the present."[58] *The Erasers* by Alain Robbe-Grillet (1953) and *Chronicle of a Death Foretold* by García Márquez (1981) employ a broken line narrative. In these two novels, the narrators start at the end (the murder), return to the past, order the events according to the broken line narration, and then come back to the beginning-end (the murder). Although the journalist and the novelist can follow the same narrative line, in these two novels the authors assimilate the news story to the pattern of Sophocles' *Oedipus Rex*, so that a banal murder reaches the dimensions of tragedy. These two novels show how literature and journalism can combine to produce a bigeneric and original work.

Narrativity emerges as the dominant arena in which the novelist and the journalist interact in their respective roles as codifiers of the message which will be transmitted to the reader. Despite the restrictions of time, space and subject placed on the journalist, García Márquez the journalist-fiction writer continues to develop the possibilities of narrative discourse in both genres; that is, from the outset, he continues to experiment with narrative discourse in his journalistic pieces and keeps adding journalistic elements to his fiction. If the news story is susceptible to a double and coetaneous journalistic and literary development, it can also be narrated journalistically in a short story or novel, or novelistically in a news story, article or chronicle. This overlapping leads to the concept of the hybridized text, that is, the journalistic-literary text, which coincides with the development of García Márquez as a hyphenated writer. Certainly, some of García Márquez's texts are more recognizably literary than journalistic, but the large majority fall into the hybrid category in which the author functions as a journalistic-literary codifier in the production of the message.

As for the position of the journalist and the novelist vis-a-vis the decodifier or audience, the journalist, unlike the novelist, must possess a much more exact idea of the real reader because he usually targets a specific audience. The novelist, on the other hand, must deal with a much more diverse reading public, and sometimes he resorts to the idea of the implied reader; that is, the image of the reader to which he wishes to direct his work. The journalist and the novelist can try to elicit a particular reaction in the reader, but neither one can control this reaction with absolute certainty. The journalist and the novelist use narrative discourse to convey the specific configuration of the message-reaction.

With respect to the feedback which a novel or news story generates, the writer must have some knowledge of how the receiver processes the information. In journalism, since the same message can be disseminated through various channels---like radio and television---and the message is in general more specific and restricted, feedback is also more direct and immediate. The diversity of the novelist's audience and the multifaceted "message" of the novel complexify the question of feedback. Nevertheless, the messages in both genres pass through the same steps in the communication process.

Although one type of novel or subgenre of journalism may dominate at a given moment, none of these classifications has been able to impose itself as the final definition of either genre. The same proliferation of subgenres and the absence of overall definitions, confirm that the novel and journalism are open systems of human communication which constantly evolve and adapt to the new channels that are developing to transmit their messages. The one constant is the fundamental need to use narrative discourse to convey the message. This interfacial point between journalism and the novel represents the most solid link and the most productive focus for examining the work of a journalist-fiction writer. In a world filled with the almost infinite voices striving to communicate, narrative discourse is constantly transmitting these voices to different receivers through a wide variety of channels. Within this incredible sonorous and written tumult, journalism and the novel represent key players. In this vast network of human communication, as Bakhtin so simply and eloquently states, "there is neither a first nor a last word and there are no limits to the dialogic context (it extends into the boundless past and the boundless future). Even *past* meanings, that is, those born in the dialogue of past centuries, can never be stable (finalized, ended once and for all)---they will always change (be renewed) in the process of subsequent, future development of the dialogue."[59] The one constant remains narrative discourse, which constitutes the central focus of our analysis of the work of García Márquez, journalist-fiction writer.

Notes

1.   The stories are "The Third Resignation" (*El Espectador*, Bogotá, September 13, 1947, "Weekend" section, 8), "Eva Is Inside Her Cat" (*El Espectador*, Bogotá, October 25, 1947, "Weekend" section, 8), and the following year, "Tubal-Cain Forges a Star" (*El Espectador*, January 17, "Weekend" section, 8). García Márquez's first journalistic piece appeared in *El Universal* of Cartagena on May 21, 1948, pages 4 and 8. The short text deals with the effect of the curfew on Cartagena.

2.   Carmen Rabell, *Periodismo y ficción en Crónica de una*

muerte anunciada (Santiago: Instituto Profesional del Pacífico, 1985), 14. Translation is mine.

3.	Aníbal González, "The Ends of the Text: Journalism in the Fiction of Gabriel García Márquez," in: Julio Ortega, *Gabriel García Márquez and the Powers of Fiction* (Austin: Univ. of Texas Press, 1988), 62.

4.	Raúl Rivadeneira Prada, *Periodismo: La teoría general de los sistemas y la ciencia de la comunicación* (México: Editorial Trillas, 1977), 16-17. All translations are mine.

5.	Tzvetan Todorov, *Mikhail Bakhtin: The Dialogical Principle*, trans. Wlad Godzich (Minneapolis: The Univ. of Minnesota Press, 1984), 82.

6.	Tzvetan Todorov, *The Dialogical Principle*, 82.

7.	M. M. Bakhtin, *Speech Genres & Other Late Essays*, Trans. Vern W. McGee (Austin: Univ. of Texas Press, 1986), 60.

8.	M. M. Bakhtin, *Speech Genres*, 62.

9.	M. M. Bakhtin, *Speech Genres*, 62.

10.	In Mario Vargas Llosa's novel, *The Storyteller*, trans. Helen Lane (New York: Farrar, Straus and Giroux, 1989), the unnamed narrator's best friend, Saúl Zuratas, who feels a profound fascination for the Machiguenga Indians of the Peruvian Amazon, abandons modern society and returns to primary orality. He becomes the travelling "storyteller" responsible for transmitting and disseminating the collective memory of Machiguengas. This novel offers one of the few examples in which a character returns to a society with primary orality.

11.	Walter J. Ong, *Orality and Literacy: The Technologizing of the Word* (New York: Methuen, 1983), 136.

12.   *The New Journalism (With an Anthology)*, ed. Tom Wolfe and E. W. Johnson (New York: Harper & Row, 1973), 25.

13.   Aníbal González, "The Ends of the Text," 62.

14.   Aníbal González, "The Ends of the Text," 62-3.

15.   Aníbal González, 63.

16.   Tom Wolfe, *The New Journalism*, 15.

17.   M. M. Bakhtin, *Speech Genres & Other Essays*, 152.

18.   Tom Wolfe, *The New Journalism*, 31.

19.   Tom Wolfe, *The New Journalism*, 31-2.

20.   Gérard Genette, *Narrative Discourse Revisited*, trans. Jane E. Lewin (Ithaca: Cornell UP, 1988), 8.

21.   Gérard Genette, *Narrative Discourse Revisited*, 8.

22.   Gerald Prince, *Dictionary of Narratology* (Lincoln: Univ. of Nebraska Press, 1989), 65.

23.   Gerald Prince, 65.

24.   Gerald Prince, 65.

25.   Genette, *Narrative Discourse Revisited*, 8.

26.   Steven Cohan and Linda M. Shires, *Telling Stories: A Theoretical Analysis of Narrative Fiction* (London: Routledge, 1988), 119-20.

27.   *Telling Stories*, 120.

28.   *Telling Stories*, 121.

29.   *Telling Stories*, 123.

30. *Telling Stories*, 124.

31. Roland Barthes, *S/Z*, Trans. Richard Miller (New York: Hill and Wang, 1974), 20.

32. Cohan, *Telling Stories*, 128.

33. Roland Barthes, *S/Z*, 20.

34. Gérard Genette, *Palimpsestes: La Littérature au Second Degré* (Paris: Editions du Seuil, 1982), 7. All translations are mine.

35. Genette, *Palimpsestes*, 8.

36. Lucien Dällenbach, "Intertexte et autotexte," *Poétique*, 27 (1976), 282. Translation is mine.

37. Dällenbach, "Intertexte et autotexte," 283.

38. Genette, *Palimpsestes*, 9.

39. Genette, *Palimpsestes*, 10.

40. Genette, *Palimpsestes*, 11.

41. Genette, *Palimpsestes*, 12.

42. Genette, *Palimpsestes*, 11.

43. Genette, *Palimpsestes*, 15.

44. Raúl Rivadeneira Prada, *Periodismo: La teoría general de los sistemas y la ciencia de la comunicación*, 34.

45. Raúl Rivadeneira Prada, *La opinión pública: Análisis, estructura y métodos para su estudio* (México: Editorial Trillas, 1976), 166. Translations are mine.

46. Rivadeneira Prada, *La opinión pública*, 166.

47.   Rivadeneira Prada, *La opinión pública*, 166.

48.   Rivadeneira Prada, 167.

49.   Rivadeneira Prada, 167.

50.   Rivadeneira Prada, 167.

51.   Rivadeneira Prada, 167.

52.   Rivadeneira Prada details a variety of news sources, including rumor, the version, news leak, off the record, press alerts, press releases, public relations, information sheets, hand-outs, press conferences, official statements to the press, interviews, expert opinion and polls. *Periodismo*, 76-90.

53.   The following discussion of the news item is based on Aníbal González's presentation in "The Ends of the Text," 68.

54.   Richard Weiner, *Webster's New World Dictionary of Media and Communications* (New York: Simon & Schuster, 1990), 402.

55.   Roland Barthes, *Critical Essays*, trans. Richard Howard (Evanston: Northwestern UP, 1972), 191.

56.   Renato Prada Oropeza, *El lenguaje narrativo: Prolegómenos para una semiótica narrativa* (Costa Rica: Editorial Universitaria Centroamericana, 1979), 231. Translation is mine.

57.   Gerald Prince, *Dictionary of Narratology*, 5 and 77.

58.   Alexis Márquez Rodríguez, *La comunicación impresa: Teoría y práctica del lenguaje periodístico* (Caracas: Ediciones Centauro, 1976), 132. Translation is mine.

59.   M. M. Bakhtin, *Speech Genres & Other Late Essays*, 170.

Chapter 2

Journalistic Peregrinations I: Coast, Costeños, Cartagena, El Universal, 1949-1950

Chronologically, García Márquez's first journalistic piece appeared eight months after the publication of his first short story. This slight time difference concerning the actual "beginning" of García Márquez's career only reinforces the idea that his writing does not recognize any first or last words, that it is constantly evolving. Even more important is the fact that his first stories were published in the limited space of the newspaper which is governed by strict formal criteria. Normally, the newspaper column and columnist suggest a series of feature articles which appear regularly, deal with a specific subject, and are written by the same person whose ideas and beliefs coincide with those of the newspaper. García Márquez's journalistic debut as a columnist presents a different picture: "It is not easy to detect the different basic structures of a newspaper column which, like "Another Story" in Cartagena and "La Jirafa" in Barranquilla, allowed the inclusion of absolutely everything that the journalist wanted to write in it, from a formal point of view, without, it seems, a chief editor calling his attention to any style book. The fact that the journalist in question lacked any formal training and, that, presumably, he only knew that the column had to be well written, do not help explain the situation."[1] Confronted with this restricted blank space, the young writer may have felt a little disoriented. García Márquez's atypical debut in journalism requires framing the context in which he started to write.

García Márquez never seems to have suffered from the proverbial fear of the "blank page," or, in this case, from "the blank space of the newspaper column," when his only criterium was that he had to "write well." This situation was quite prevalent in the Colombian press: "Moreover, this thematic variety of García Márquez's columns corresponds to the general practice in the Colombian press, then as well as now, of assigning those spaces

31

in the newspaper to people who 'write well' and who, except in rare cases, do not oppose the newspaper's philosophy. Consequently, in these authentic fiefdoms, the reader can find almost any topic: a commentary about the mayor, a film review or a social note."[2] Beyond García Márquez's more stimulating work as a columnist, his labors also included writing headlines, correcting teletype copy, and his involvement with the layout staff which was an "apprenticeship for the job from the ground up that would certainly be useful to him in the future."[3] Apparently, this anonymous work partly fulfilled the function of a style book, and the enigmatic chief editor of *El Universal*, Clemente Manuel Zabala, must have had an important influence on García Márquez: "Zabala would unmercifully correct the notes of García Márquez, including his anonymous ones, and he would not hesitate to cross out and rewrite whenever he decided that the writing of the novice journalist did not measure up to his standards."[4] As a result, García Márquez's training in journalism not only afforded him the opportunity to experiment within the elastic formal and thematic constraints of the column, but also involved him in the more anonymous aspects of the newspaper which undoubtedly helped him develop his style and techniques.

The prevailing censorship also played a role in García Márquez's journalistic debut, and it was still in force when he left for Europe in 1955 as a foreign corespondent for *El Espectador*. After the "Bogotazo," the assassination of Jorge Eliécer Gaitán on April 9, 1948, the government promulgated Decree 1271 which imposed censorship. In 1949, Decree 3521 established prior censorship, and Decree 3580 set up the Office of Prior Censorship. This trend continued to intensify as the yoke of censorship grew more and more restrictive until 1957 when it was finally lifted.[5] If censorship exercised a more oblique influence when García Márquez embarked on his journalistic career, it would become one of the cultural codes that he would confront as an investigative reporter for *El Espectador*. Above all, García Márquez would endeavor to dialogize censorship and assimilate it to the other codes which are embedded in his journalistic pieces. Censorship is a discourse which cannot be eliminated without falsifying reality.

Besides reiterating in many interviews that the ultimate source of creation is reality, García Márquez also affirms that reality does not end with the price of tomatoes. From a retrospective point of view, these repeated declarations could be construed as some of the stock cliches that he offers to the press, part of the legendary aura that now surrounds the famous Nobel laureate. Nevertheless, if these same remarks are placed in the early phase of his career, they take on new significance. García Márquez's belief that reality is the final arbiter of creation reflects the attitude of another famous journalist-fiction writer, Ernest Hemingway.

Hemingway not only viewed reality as the ultimate source of creation, but also transformed it into the central quest of his characters: "In writing for a newspaper you told what happened and, with one trick and another, you communicated the emotion aided by the element of timeliness which gives a certain emotion to any account of something that has happened on that day; but the real thing, the sequence of motion and fact which made the emotion and which would be as valid in a year or in ten years or, with luck and if you stated it purely enough, always, was beyond me and I was working very hard to try and get it."[6] While Hemingway and García Márquez consider reality as the authentic source of their work, their respective approaches differ in significant ways. García Márquez believes that reality also contains magic, fantastic, mythic elements and superstitions, all of which play a key role in the daily life of people. Everything is already present and the writer does not have to invent anything. Reality is already multifaceted, overflowing with all the raw materials that García Márquez needs for his journalistic-literary windmill.

Hemingway's concept of reality represents a conquest, and he is always endeavoring to close the gap between the fleeting immediacy of experience and its description. This is what he calls "the real thing," and, in the majority of his novels, the characters, through their extreme visual intensity, try to capture the real thing in all its purity. In an interview in *The Paris Review*, Hemingway said bluntly that "the most essential gift for a good writer is a built-in shockproof, shit detector."[7] What distinguishes the two writers is that Hemingway consistently searched for stylistic transcendence, or the moment in which he could bridge the gap between experience and description to reach "the real thing." García Márquez seeks to incorporate all the components of reality because he believes that they are all equally valid.

Their different approaches to reality closely relate to the lessons in style and technique that they received and to the way in which they assimilated them.   Unlike García Márquez, who slowly developed his style and techniques without the aid of a formal style manual, Hemingway debuted as a reporter for the *Kansas City Star* which required its reporters to adhere to a set of strict stylistic norms: "Use short sentences. Use short first paragraphs.   Use vigorous English. Be positive, not negative."[8] All these elements contributed to the Hemingway style which would become the hallmark of his work and would transform American fiction.

If Hemingway applied his journalistic writing techniques directly to his fiction from the outset, García Márquez followed a more circular path. In García Márquez's writing "the real thing" became what can be called the rhetoric of particularity, in which he concentrates on ostensibly insignificant concrete details.   Once contextualized, they become indispensable components of the human context. Consequently, his writing does not exhibit a frenetic search for moments of stylistic transcendence. The human context contains an almost inexhaustible supply of particularities on which he can draw, and the rhetoric of particularity reinforces the dynamic evolution of his writing.   García Márquez has always considered literature and journalism modes of writing rather than formal and distinct genres, and they have always offered him a laboratory in which he carry out his experiments in bigeneric writing. Accordingly, the initial image of the young writer shows an inexperienced journalist, debuting as a columnist who alternates between two genres, does not possess fixed ideas about different styles, and who imitates other writers in his short stories while temporarily disavowing his personal experience as the source of his raw materials.   More importantly, journalism and literature are unbounded expanses receptive to dialogic interaction, and this situation initiates a process which will continue to evolve and change.

In an interview in 1981 concerning his novel, *Chronicle of a Death Foretold*, García Márquez again reiterated this point: "For the first time I achieved a perfect balance between journalism and literature, and that's why the book is called *Chronicle of a Death Foretold*. That supposedly bad influence that journalism has on literature isn't so certain. First of all, because I don't think anything destroys the writer, not even hunger. Secondly, because journalism helps you stay in touch with reality, which is essential for working in literature. And vice versa, because literature teaches you how to write, which is also essential for journalism. In my case, journalism was the springboard to literature, and I learned to write journalism by writing good literature."[9] García Márquez thus produced a work which reconfirmed the intimate relation between journalism and literature. The fundamental gross constituents of his themes, style and narrative techniques took shape between 1947 and 1955, and this period passes through various stages.

During the first phase of García Márquez's career as a journalist, which extends from May, 1948 to December, 1949, his signed output consists of 38 pieces published in the column "Another Story" ("Punto y aparte") of the Cartagena daily *El Universal*. From January, 1950 to December, 1952, he wrote nearly four hundred short pieces in the column "La Jirafa" (The Giraffe") for *El Heraldo* of Barranquilla. Although his literary production from 1947 to 1955 is not as extensive, it nevertheless demonstrates a slow but progressive evolution. His literary efforts include fifteen short stories, a novel, *Leaf Storm* (finished in 1951 and published in 1955), and a series of notes for a projected novel entitled *The House*. Although he never completed this novel, these "archeological finds not only contain a considerable number of suggested, adumbrated or explicit prefigurations and prophecies of his future works, but also of works which would be written some twenty years later.[10]

The predominance of journalism relates to other factors than García Márquez's personal preferences. In 1947, he initiated his law studies at the Universidad Nacional in Bogotá, but it closed following the assassination of the Jorge Eliécer Gaitán. In May, 1948, García Márquez traveled to Cartagena where the university remained open, with the intention of continuing his legal studies. In Cartagena he met the doctor and writer, Manuel Zapata Olivella, who, according to García Márquez, took him to the offices of a recently established newspaper. García Márquez continued to work for the newspaper while he proceeded with his studies, but he abandoned them completely in 1950.

Beyond the 38 signed pieces, he was involved in the anonymous work of editing and rewriting many other articles that cannot be identified. Although the biographical details of his twenty months with *El Universal* remain incomplete, one event stands out: his first encounters with a group of intellectuals which would come to be known as the "Group of Barranquilla."[11] His link with this group introduced him to writers like Ernest Hemingway, William Faulkner and Virginia Woolf, who in turn opened up new channels for his writing. After moving to Barranquilla, García Márquez worked for *El Heraldo* from January, 1950 to December, 1952. From January, 1953 to February, 1954, he worked in several different jobs, including an itinerant book salesman and a "brief and intense stint as the chief editor of the evening edition of *El Nacional*."[12] García Márquez then moved to Bogotá where he worked for *El Espectador* from February, 1954 to July, 1955. The Bogotá phase marked the entry of the young writer into investigative reporting. Consequently, the first stage of García Márquez's career is marked by an intensive journalistic production, a less extensive literary output and his introduction to authors who would help determine the configuration of his vision and literary style. Above all, this initial stage represents a decisive step in which García Márquez begins to develop the primary narrative, stylistic and thematic elements which will shape his writing, especially his fiction.

Hugging the Coast: **El Universal** *and García Márquez the Columnist*

The relative absence of formal restraints for writing his column and García Márquez's minimal professional training in journalism, preclude a study of his first pieces according to specific set of journalistic criteria. A chronological study also yields unsatisfactory results because neither the ideological content nor the style of the column conforms to any discernible pattern. When García Márquez undertook his assignment to write the column, the only requirement was to "write well." Moreover, faced with the daily task of writing a column with no set focus, he would sometimes have to improvise subjects. A perusal of these pieces confirms their thematic and stylistic heterogeneity. The topics include "inconsequential events of regional, national and foreign origin (the cable as a source of the column), literary texts, biographical vignettes, slices of life pieces, social notes and extravagant reflections."[13]   Other themes involve politics, violence, the Coast and its culture, the city, music, Europe, the United States and personal notes. The personal pieces were perhaps the result of his work as staff editor and other anonymous tasks he performed for the newspaper, yet it "appears undeniable that to write his column García Márquez was forced to resort to personal notes, 'including his secret writer's papers.'"[14]

The censorship established shortly after the assassination of Jorge Eliécer Gaitán also influenced the content of the column. The "Another Story" column of *El Universal* and "La Jirafa" of *El Heraldo* "were written in the context of intimidation that all censorship entails, and that situation not only determined the selection of many themes for the column but also its form and style which cannot be naively considered as basically humorous."[15]   Despite the censorship, the antidogmatic temperament of the costeños and their mistrust of the cachacos signified that the actual application of the censorship was less severe. The best proof of this situation is the constant presence of "mamagallismo" in García Márquez's pieces, this irrepressible and permanent sense of humor in the face of life's solemnity and seriousness, qualities which García Márquez considers the patrimony of the cachacos. Pedro Sorela adds that *El Universal* and *El Heraldo* were "Republican newspapers---that is, part of the establishment---, which, if they criticized the arbitrary actions of despotic governments within certain limits, in the best tradition of the Latin American free press, would not have easily tolerated the presence of a Communist as a member of its staff or as a writer occupying the privileged position of a columnist."[16]

Since García Márquez never attempts to circumvent the discourse of censorship by eliminating it artificially, he will oppose it on a dialogical, discursive and narrative plane.   Indeed, censorship, which had continued to tighten its grip since its enactment in 1948, and the development of García Márquez's career as a journalist, were on a collision course from the outset, and they would meet face to face in 1955 when he would publish his fourteen part series on the adventures of the sailor Luis Alejandro Velasco in *El Espectador*. Although García Márquez's early journalistic pieces present a potpourri of subjects and themes, they activate certain aspects of his writing that we defined in Chapter 1. While the formal aspects of journalism contribute to the study of these pieces, Genette's transtextual categories serve as the primary critical framework for analyzing them on the textual level.   We also group the texts according to certain themes to facilitate a comparative study. This global perspective allows us to introduce other forms of textual criticism and to analyze their journalistic aspects. We focus on ten texts divided into three categories: 1) three political columns with hypertextual relations; 2) two literary pieces with metatextual relations; and 3) five cultural texts with intertextual relations.

Political Texts With Hypertextual Relations

In García Márquez's first journalistic piece, like others which deal with politics, he establishes a hypertextual relation with censorship: "We inhabitants of the city had grown accustomed to the metallic voice which announced the curfew. The clock of the Boca del Puente, towering over the city again in its clean, whitewashed convalescence, had lost its familiar appearance, its irreplaceable value as an old friend."[17] Although this poetized opening (metallic voice, its whitewashed convalescence) fulfills the requirement of "writing well" as García Márquez interprets it, the language bears little resemblance to standard journalese. The mention of the curfew not only acknowledges the censorship but also the authority which imposes it. While the author neither refers directly to censorship nor speaks of it as a hypotext, the curfew serves to concretize it. By identifying with the city's inhabitants, the author adopts their perspective when he describes the clock of Boca del Puente. In this Cartagena overflowing with history, the author draws on the history code when he notes that the same clock which has lost its familiar place, also serves to announce the curfew. This opening also addresses the hypotext of poetry, and especially the movement known as *piedracielismo* in Colombia, which sought new images to defamiliarize reality.[18] Defamiliarization makes "the familiar strange by impeding automatic, habitual ways of perceiving."[19] If García Márquez adopts the same perspective as the man on the street to look at the clock of Boca del Puente, they clearly do not view it in the same way. The author works within the symbolic code, establishing a binary opposition between the two functions of the clock, and he thus opens the way for his meditation on time. García Márquez will continue to develop the technique of defamiliarization in his work, but in this text he does not naturalize the defamiliarized reality so that his readers can accept it.

During the curfew, time is controlled by a new mechanical system, "that slow, agonizing progression, which kept pushing the hours against a familiar border which was, in turn, the terrible shore where our freedom gave way" (77). The disorientation and fear caused by curfew materialize in the images of temporal dislocation. Everyday at noon, the shrill sound which announces the lifting of the curfew recalls "another big, confused and absurd rooster who had lost its sense of time" (77). The silence which falls over the city after the signal resembles "that deep, imperturbable silence which precedes great catastrophes" (77). The human context of this situation remains collective and rather abstract, as if focalized from the outside. The allusion to Sir

Francis Drake, who had attacked Cartagena, underscores the repression and danger associated with the curfew: "Submerged in the silence, we only heard the rebellious, impotent sound of our breathing, as if Francis Drake were still out there in the bay, with his boarding ships" (77).[20]

Time remains historical, and the curfew corresponds to the one "which the English heard after the first bombings in London. The same as in Warsaw" (78). The fear generated by the curfew is depersonalized, and the reader feels detached from the human context. After noting that the curfew has not sounded since yesterday, the author again resorts to facile, literary images to express waiting for the "dawn smelling of woods, of damp earth that will come like a new, sporty and modern-day Sleeping Beauty" (78). Although historical time dominates in this piece, the reader senses the presence of another time governed by human experience. García Márquez is already tampering with the strict spatiotemporal limits of journalism by introducing anachronies which allude to other historical events. While the effects of the curfew extend beyond Cartagena, they still do not spill over into the transhistorical framework to become a universal experience. Nevertheless, the presence of anachronies also reveals the importance of narrative discourse in carrying out this project.

In another piece of June 22, 1948, the author presents a bittersweet, war-peace lamentation which registers a profound feeling of betrayal couched in poetico-rhetorical language. The hypotexts of censorship and poetry continue to occupy the author's attention: "We are in agreement, my friend and comrade. We, the men of this generation, which today is approaching its maturity, we did not know the creature of the violence" (101). The author poetizes his confrontation with the official world and its heteroglossia. He intertextualizes with the official world by employing a series of images drawn from the history books which present Colombia's past in glorious, patriotic terms: "We knew that peace was the truth because it filled all the books which colored our perception of things" (101). These books presented pictures of peace found "in the working class, in the soldier's letter, in the music of the turbines, in the prow of the ships, in the slavery of bread and in the freedom of horses" (101). While the author is writing within the symbolic code, apparently he does not know how to assimilate censorship to his own discourse. The poetic images defamiliarize reality, but not within the cultural norms of the readers.

The author continues to use the same poetico-rhetorical language, but it undergoes what Bakhtin calls refraction: "Every word is like a ray of light on a trajectory to both an object and a receiver. Both paths are strewn with previous claims that slow up, distort, refract the intention of the word."[21] Before reaching the reader, words always pass through different zones which refract their meaning. In this piece, the reader passes from the peace to the war zone, and the same poetic images acquire a different meaning. The war zone "has the smell of a barricade" and "the shadow of the bayonets" (101-02). Censorship and political violence characterize this zone now, and the words of Tacitus take on an ironic tone: "A bad peace is still worse than war" (102).

In another note of June 24, 1948, the coercion of censorship manifests itself in the poeticization of a fallen Liberal leader: "Upright, erect and magnificent, Braulio Henao Blanco has fallen victim to the blazing fury of violence" (102). The text functions on one level as a pastiche of the grandiloquent, rhetorical style appropriate for eulogizing the spirit of the man whereas, on another level, it parodies this rhetorical form. This would be valid if the rest of the text were not also dominated by an overabundance of poetic images: "In the same city where he erected his barriers of justice, where his gleaming words defended with lucid strokes the sturdy anatomy of democracy, here his slumping body fell and his last outcry rose up like a prophetic proclamation" (102). The author imagines him "commanding his armies, ordering his agrarian legions, united with the group of liberators who clamor for justice, who seek peace, harmony and understanding, so that men of good will not disappear" (102-03).

The somewhat indiscriminate combination and handling of the textual codes in these political columns detract from their readability. This does not mean that they are devoid of any literary or journalistic value since García Márquez will progressively transcend the traditional boundaries of journalism. His indecision about the censorship hypotext and the excess of images from the poetry hypotext result in an unwieldy combination of textual codes that give censorship a more prominent role than it deserves. Obviously, García Márquez has not been able to integrate the heteroglossia of censorship into his writing because he does not challenge it directly in these pieces. It could be argued that the hypotexts are not visible enough to warrant their use, but, as Genette affirms, transtextuality must not be considered "as a class of texts but rather as an aspect of textuality."[22]   He adds that hypertextuality "is evidently a universal aspect (almost to the same extent) of literariness: there exists no literary work which does not, to some degree and in accordance with its readers, evoke another one and, in this sense, all works are hypertextual."[23] Consequently, hypertextuality not only demonstrates that its reach is longer than the other transtextual categories, but also that any textual classification, however exclusive it may claim to be, ends up including the others. The author resorts to the official language of eulogy to parody it and communicate the ideas of Henao Blanco. This parodic hypertextuality enables him to break the silence imposed by the death of Braulio Henao Blanco and to reach the reader through a language interspersed with poetico-rhetorical images appropriate for the occasion.

While the author's principal aim is to reaffirm the positive ideas that Braulio embodied, he indirectly tries to expose the emptiness of his eulogy: "His name now has the taste of stone. Braulio Henao Blanco, citizen of eternity" (103).   This text corresponds to what Bakhtin labels *dialogized language* (as opposed to *undialogized language* which is authoritative and monological) in which "everything means, is understood, as part of a greater whole---there is a constant interaction between meanings, all of which have the potential of conditioning others."[24]   Since a tension between centripetal and centrifugal forces characterizes heteroglossia, the appearance of this column one day after the death of Blanco places it at the center of a situation which generates different discourses. Censorship and authority act as centripetal forces trying to impose an undialogized language (the depoliticized eulogy), while Blanco's death and his ideas serve as centrifugal forces which dislodge the eulogy and link it to dialogized language. The author taps this dialogized language to denounce the absurdity of his death and to provide a filter through which his ideas can be communicated. When the author says that "in the obscure region of death I see him leading his illuminated birds" (102), he produces what J. L. Austin calls a "performative utterance" (the description of an action amounts to accomplishing that action), for the "illuminated birds" change into the readers who will continue to hear his ideas enunciated.[25] García Márquez thus not only shows an awareness of a range of different languages but also the ability to adapt them to his own purposes.

Literary Texts With Metatextual Relations

The open space of the column also engenders metatextual relations in the form of "literary" criticism. In "The Life and Novels of Poe (Commentaries)" (October 7, 1949), the word "commentaries" in parentheses suggests the copresence of three hypotexts that comprise the metatextual relation: 1) the literary work of García Márquez seen in relation to certain traits of the life and work of Poe; 2) the meta- metatext of American criticism that stands in binary opposition to the first hypotext; and 3) the metatext of the indirect criticism that García Márquez levels at the censorship imposed on the newspaper. In the metatextual relation the text refers to another text "without necessarily quoting it (calling it forth), and even, in the most extreme case, without naming it."[26]

To naturalize and situate Poe within the cultural codes of the readers, the author employs the hermeneutic code. The opening sentence creates an enigma which the reader must start to decipher: "Paul Valéry spoke of Edgar Allen Poe as a genius who was unknown or forgotten by his own peers" (139). García

Márquez considers the first sentence of his works a start-up lab which "unfailingly has the power to capture the reader's attention, although later on this action may remain unfulfilled."[27] By situating Poe between "unknown" and "forgotten" the author doubles the enigma which Poe represented for his contemporaries. The rhetoric of particularity establishes the reality of the cryptic writer by portraying his agonizing death in a Baltimore hospital "racked by the specters of 'delirium tremens'" (139). The author immediately inverts this image by returning to the hermeneutic code, because "American literature does not record any similar case" (139). He completes his defamiliarization of the reality surrounding Poe by asserting that "the Americans lost their sense of mystery" (139). Poe is thus transformed into a mystery wrapped in an enigma.

The successive transformations of Poe not only arouse the reader's interest in the hermeneutic code, but also link him to the other two metatexts. Despite Poe's peculiar literary baggage, his work "responds to a profound human bond which cannot be ignored in the appreciation of any author" (139). The author renaturalizes Poe by placing him in the framework of universal literature. Poe retains his enigmatic aura only for those who are linked to the meta- metatext of American criticism and, in a more implicit way, for the censorship which does not tolerate anything or anyone who appears strange, abnormal and does not conform to its rigid norms of reality. For the young García Márquez there is nothing mysterious in Poe's work which constitutes "the personal record of the neurosis which conditioned all aspects of his psychological universe" (139). Indeed, García Márquez, in his early short stories, investigated the same universe of neurotic and psychological states. Consequently, García Márquez ascribes considerable importance to Poe's childhood in the eventual shape of his work. Because of an injury that Poe may have suffered in childhood, "the sum total of his work, its tragic and heart-rending ambience, revolve around that vital failure" (141). Although García Márquez's early literary work drew its inspiration from outside sources, at least he could recognize the importance of childhood in another's work.

He juxtaposes this metatext to that of American criticism, and he even quotes a critic named Lewisohn, who denigrates and condemns Poe's work. According to Lewisohn, Poe's work not only exceeds the bounds of reality but, worse yet, it creates a self-enclosed universe which detaches itself from the real world. In the same neurosis which, according to García Márquez, produces Poe's profound humanity, Lewisohn finds "the reason for this tendency to take refuge in the fantastic" (140). The author undercuts this metatext by hypertextualizing the work of Poe with those of other great writers who also suffered from different maladies: "It would be superfluous to cite the cases of Dostoevsky, an epileptic, or that of Franz Kafka, a genius who was racked by abstinence and tuberculosis" (140-01).

The metatext of criticism that the author addresses to censorship manifests itself indirectly. In general, censorship operates within narrow boundaries, and it feels threatened by anything that may undermine its monolithic conception of reality. To counteract this official reality, the author continuously renaturalizes the abnormal, linking Poe's strange literary baggage to the idea that his disease not only constitutes the source of his eccentricity and his "moving human condition," but also the driving force of his creativity. The same defamiliarization of reality thus acts to naturalize Poe as a writer and to denounce the rigid norms of his critics. Defamiliarization also enables García Márquez to express his firm opposition to the dehumanizing censorship when he says that Poe's situation "is also a human condition capable of being projected into his work, with results as respectable and startling as those of Balzac, Dostoevsky or Cervantes" (140).

The interplay of metatexts not only corresponds to the open format of the column, but also reflects García Márquez's willingness to experiment. Paradoxically, this attitude stems more from the lack of formal journalistic criteria than from the concerted effort to develop his writing. Nevertheless, each metatext successively parodies the other, resulting in an open text which does not draw a definite conclusion. This series of parodies and counterparodies combines to create a continuous dialogue. This type of text can be called a metaparody.[28]   Metaparodies "frequently work by first parodying an original, then parodying the parody of the original."[29]   The author begins by parodying the enigma of Poe, makes him enigmatic again, and then parodies the literary criticism and the censorship that consider Poe "strange," "abnormal" and, finally, a pariah. The last sentence of the piece does not conclude but opens the way for the multiple interpretations engendered by the metaparody: "Hopefully this first centennial of his death will be a decisive moment in the fair and necessary appraisal of Edgar Allen Poe" (141). This analysis does not imply that the author, in this initial stage, is *intentionally* creating this type of text, since its form is determined more by extratextual factors. Nevertheless, the presence of metaparody comes as no surprise because mamagallismo is inherent to García Márquez's costeño mind-set, and he himself will play with the hermeneutic code and expectations of his readers.

The author establishes a metatextual relation with his own work in his literary commentary on *Initial Ceremony* written by a young Cartagena novelist, George Lee Bisswell Cotes (December 22, 1948). This metatext transforms itself into a metaparody; that is, a parody of the parodic commentary on the novel.   In metaparody, ambiguity plays an important role, and it takes the form of a parody-counterparody dialogue. Therefore, the choice of a metatextual relation must correspond generically to the parodied text.   Moreover, the text deploys a series of hermeneutic resonances about the young Cartagena novelist which the reader must decipher. One of the genres of metaparody is the rhetorical paradox, which is "the praise of something regarded as essentially unpraisable."[30]   García Márquez uses rhetorical paradox to praise this unpraisable novel, and the metaparody coincides with the idea of costeño mamagallismo.

The most interesting facet of George Lee Bisswell Cotes is not his novel but his onomastic peculiarity: "The best thing that has happened to George Lee Bisswell Cotes is to have been born with a name which is difficult to pronounce in a country where extreme climates predominate" (879). Indeed, nowhere in his commentary does the author discuss the content of the novel, and he prefers to situate Bisswell Cotes in the onomastic paradise of those authors whose names capture our attention, "alongside Zangwilly, S. S. Van Dyne, Bjoérsen, Hofmaustall, Sullonphaa and other masters in the hallowed realm of difficult names" (879).[31]. If his difficult name surprises people, the author continues to defamiliarize the person of the young novelist.

Despite the strange atmosphere which envelops him, the author endeavors to naturalize Bisswell Cotes by explaining that his behavior relates to his method of writing: "Bisswell himself was explaining to me later that---according to the way he understands it---it is a good idea to record experience as it is happening. The chapter should directly transfer real life to the universe of the novel, without concern for continuity, flowing with living sap, without indulging the prerogatives of the imaginative faculties" (880). The metatext of García Márquez's work intervenes at this point because, according to him, he wrote in the same way at the start of his career: "At the beginning, when I was learning my craft, I wrote jubilantly, almost irresponsibly. I remember, in those days, I could easily write four, five, even ten pages of a book after I'd finished work on the newspaper around two or three in the morning."[32]

Consciously or not, García Márquez changes his commentary-parody of Bisswell Cotes' novel into a metaparody of his own literary production of the period. As for the rhetorical aspect of Bisswell Cotes' novel, the author affirms that it suffers from the "practical, pompous, asphyxiating and cheap rhetoric that governs all the movements of human activity, and which every good writer---by convention---takes it upon himself to falsify in order to imbue his work with what some call NATURALNESS and others, PATHETIC REALISM" (881). In retrospect, this judgment not only shows the wide disparity between his enthusiastic evaluation of Poe and his mistrust of his own personal experience as a source of his work, but also indicates the embryonic state of his literary work. Apparently, Bisswell Cotes' novel is unpraisable, but to avoid denigrating it completely, the author praises the novelist by giving him lessons which will prevent him from writing another similar novel: "I am sure that in two or three years George Lee Bisswell Cotes [will recognize] the obstacles that grandiloquence, exaggerated onomatopoeic meaning and discursive luxuriance constituted for the perfect execution of his work. He will understand that he has written a novel of two hundred pages about something which deserves to be a good short story of two pages" (881).

The metatext turns into a metaparody of the parody of the novel of Bisswell Cotes. At one point the author asks rhetorically: "But does the writer have the right to present the different phases of his evolutionary process, including the very moment at which he finds himself in the first stages of literary barbarity?" (880). His answer refers to what Roland Barthes calls *readerly* fiction in which the reader plays a passive and intransitive role: "I am afraid so, as long as there are readers of the same frame of mind, who are capable of shivering before a mammoth's leg" (880). This type of reader, submerged in idleness and passivity, slowly fossilizes as he reads the mammoth's leg/work which has already turned into a fossil. In fact, the author has been parodying readerly fiction since the outset, and he progressively transforms Bisswell Cotes into a character from such a work. The metaparody looms in the background as a critical metatext of the literary work of García Márquez, who, apparently, is not aware of this connection.

Texts With Varied Themes and Intertextual Relations

This section includes five texts which García Márquez wrote without an assigned topic. In these columns the intertextual relation does not signify the actual presence of one text in another, but rather the allusive appearance "of an utterance whose full understanding presupposes the perception of a relation between it and another to which one or another of its inflections necessarily refers, and which otherwise could not be assimilated."[33]

In a column on the accordion (May 22, 1948), the author creates his own greguería by imitating Ramón Gómez de la Serna:

"I don't know what is so infectious about the accordion, but when we hear it our feelings come alive. Dear reader, please excuse me for opening with this aphorism" (79).[34] The author continues to develop the "life and passion" of the accordion by personifying it and converting its history into a musical soap opera: "It spent its best years in an odor filled, obscure corner of a German tavern" (79). Another intertext which emerges in this column is the code of authentic costeño culture: "The genuine accordion is the one which has taken up residence here in the Magdalena Valley" (79).

In another note of May 26, 1948, the author presents "a poetic column written in stanzas, and which allusively evokes the 'Poem Number Twenty' by Pablo Neruda."[35] As García Márquez says in the column: "It would recall *The Thousand and One Nights*. It would tell about the enchantment of the magic carpets that at the mere sound of a voice would carry man above the camels and the mountains" (81). This note demonstrates the open format of the column which permits the author to write poems in prose.

The influence of poetry appears in another column on the days of the week (June 24, 1948) in which he again intertextualizes with the greguería. Thursday is a hybrid day, "a flavorless and unheated piece of French toast time, without any other justification than that of forcing us to waste a part of our life that we could use for more useful things" (103). Like the previous pieces, the intertextual link manifests itself above all in an eidetic manner, and the author deploys a series of facile poetic images: "Several minutes will be sufficient for us to round out the warm fruit of Wednesday which is swaying in the trees of time with the indecisiveness of a pensive woman" (103). If these poetic images mark the beginning of defamiliarization which he will continue to develop, they do not contribute much to these essentially ajournalistic columns. The abundance of poetic images progressively displaces the column, and the intertextual link ends up overshadowing the column and disrupting the intertextual relation.

The most prevalent intertexts in these pieces are Caribbean culture, music, tropical heat, its vitality and mixture of races. In another note of June 17, 1948, the author presents two members of this racial amalgam: "An Indian, sitting behind a black woman, is travelling on the bus. He is a perfect example of those men--- half primitive, half civilized---who come down from the Sierra Nevada of Santa Marta carrying medicinal plants and secret formulas for good lovemaking" (97). The Indian and the black woman constitute elements of a mestizo/mulatto culture that García Márquez will continuously expand and authenticate to different diegrees in opposition to the cachaco culture.

The author shows a certain awareness of the dialogic resonances which emanate from this culture. The Indian's voice resembles a "twisted and knotted piece of hemp softened by the bucking pride of colts," while the voice of the black woman is "a diaphanous voice of filtered water" (97). The author then expresses his uncertainty before this intertext: "The two muffled, slow voices can be heard flowing through the weariness of the trip, through the silence of an absurd civilization" (97). As Pedro Sorela says: "At twenty, the author still has not adopted a 'national' stance, and does not define 'Caribbean' in the same way that he will later on."[36] García Márquez also converts the black woman and the Indian into generic figures of their respective races and still has not assimilated costeño culture to his writing.

In another column on love (July 10, 1948), the author succeeds in intertextualizing love, malady and theater. The opening sentence shows the importance that he attaches to the beginning of his texts: "Love is a malady of the liver as contagious as suicide, which is one of its mortal complications" (113). In this column various intertexts on love intersect---the soap opera, Proustian and theatrical versions of love---and this combination will reappear in his subsequent works. Love and suicide have been elevated "to the status of an emotional state" (113). Both are diseases for which science has been unable "to develop an appropriate treatment" (113). Soap opera love resides in "the languid, swooning posture of the medieval damsels who displayed their pallor through a window" (113). The "Proustitution" of love appears in its characterization as a contagious and incurable disease. What joins these two amorous intertexts is the inevitable theatricalization that they engender: "As soon as the first symptoms appear, the patient becomes impatient, invents arguments, sets up his scenery with the most complicated system of swooning scenes, literary promptings, and backdrops painted with lyrical timidity" (113).

The theatricalization of the two concepts of love leads to the idea of autotextuality. If the first two intertexts rely on referential intertextuality, or the relation of the column to other texts, the drama of love depends on an internal intertextuality; that is, the relation of the text to itself. This latter intertextuality produces an internal duplication, an autotext, or *mise en abyme,* which functions diegetically and metadiegetically within the same text.[37] The microdrama of love *literally* reduplicates the story of love as a disease and turns into "*a content citation or intratextual summary.*"[38] This autotext enables the author to address the code of popular culture, and the concomitant concept of love produced by the soap operas. The staging of the theatricalized and dramatized love also allows the author to metaparody the parody of love as a contagious malady. Finally, the author parodies a certain type of literature which presents love devoid of humor: "The result is that the greatest works of literature have no other purpose than finding the hepatic vulnerability of the reader" (113). García Márquez, the master of mamagallista inversions, will continue to link love with the boundless humor of costeño culture.

We have limited our analysis to the transtextual relations and various codes because García Márquez took full advantage of the open format of the column to write about a variety of themes and to include different genres. This situation requires concentrating on the textual level to maintain a unified critical focus. This approach thus avoids the problem of imposing a critical framework which the texts do not support. Classifying these columns according to their transtextual relations calls attention to different aspects of García Márquez's writing that he will continue to develop in the next stage of his journalistic writing for *El Heraldo* of Barranquilla. The critical parameters will keep pace with the development of the author's bigeneric writing. The uneven distribution of transtextual relations in these first pieces and the somewhat indiscriminate combination of genres show that he still has not mastered the use of narrative codes to involve the reader in the completion of the text. Concurrently, his costeño sense of humor and the defamiliarization of reality emerge as two of the gross constituents of his writing.

Notes

1.   Pedro Sorela, *El otro García Márquez: Los años difíciles* (Madrid: Mondadori, 1988), 51. All translations are mine.

2.   Pedro Sorela, 51.

3.   Pedro Sorela, 15.

4.   Sorela, 16.

5.   Gabriel Fonnegra, *La prensa en Colombia* (Bogotá: El Ancora Editores, 1984), 79-80.

6.   Ernest Hemingway, *Death in the Afternoon* (New York: Charles Scribner's Sons, 1960), 2.

7.   Shelley Fisher Fishkin, *From Fact to Fiction: Journalism & Imaginative Writing in America* (Oxford: Oxford UP, 1985), 137.

8.   Charles A. Fenton, *The Apprenticeship of Ernest Hemingway: The Early Years* (New York: The New American Library of World Literature, 1961), 35.

9.   Adelaida López de Martínez, rev. of *Chronicle of a Death Foretold* by Gabriel García Márquez, *Chasqui*, X. 2-3 (February-May, 1981), 72. Translation is mine.

10.   Pedro Sorela, *El otro García Márquez*, 67.

11.   Jacques Gilard states that García Márquez most likely started to associate with the Group of Barranquilla in December, 1949. See page 13 of Gabriel García Márquez, *Obra periodística Vol. I: Textos costeños*, ed. Jacques Gilard (Barcelona: Bruguera, 1981).

12.   Pedro Sorela, *El otro García Márquez*, 25. Sorela adds that "although no copies of *El Nacional* exist for those months, all evidence indicates that those months involved intense work in which Cepeda and García Márquez would stay locked up in the newspaper offices, carefully monitoring the whole process. García Márquez does not recall having signed anything. The work did not last very long: some three months for García Márquez, and perhaps several weeks for Cepeda Samudio. This was the last work that García Márquez performed as a journalist on the Coast" (25).

13.   Pedro Sorela, 28.

14.   Pedro Sorela, 29.

15.   Sorela, 27.

16.   Sorela, 47.

17.   Gabriel García Márquez, *Obra periodística, Vol. I: Textos costeños*, ed. Jacques Gilard (Barcelona: Bruguera, 1981), 77. All other quotes will come from this edition and page numbers will be given in parentheses. All translations are mine unless otherwise indicated.

18.   According to Fernando Ayala Poveda, "piedracielismo brought together a number of poets grouped around a collection of notebooks called *Piedra y cielo*. Around the 1930s, an anthology of Spanish poetry was circulated in Colombia which sparked the interest of Jorge Rojas, Eduardo Carranza, Carlos Martín, Gerardo Valencia, Arturo Camacho Ramírez, Darío Samper and Tomás Vargas Osorio. The principal model was taken by Jorge Rojas from a book by Juan Ramón Jiménez entitled *Piedra y cielo*. The group took shape from 1935 to 1939 and lasted until 1960." *Manual de*

literatura colombiana (Bogotá: Educar Editores, 1984), 171. Translation is mine.

19.   Gerald Prince, *A Dictionary of Narratology* (Lincoln: Univ. of Nebraska Press, 1989), 18. Kenrick Mose provides an exhaustive study of defamiliarization in the work of García Márquez in his book, *Defamiliarization in the Work of Gabriel García Márquez From 1947-1967* (Lewiston, New York: The Edwin Mellen Press, 1989).

20.   Sir Francis Drake (1541-1596), the famous English navigator, sacked Cartagena in 1585.

21.   M. M. Bakhtin, *The Dialogic Imagination: Four Essays*, trans. Caryl Emerson and Michael Holquist (Austin: Univ. of Texas Press, 1981), 432.

22.   Gérard Genette, *Palimpsestes: La Littérature au Second Degré* (Paris: Editions du Seuil, 1982), 15. All translations are mine.

23.   Gérard Genette, *Palimpsestes*, 16.

24.   Bakhtin, *The Dialogic Imagination*, 426.

25.   Oswald Ducrot and Tzvetan Todorov, *Encyclopedic Dictionary of the Sciences of Language*, trans. Catherine Porter (Baltimore: The Johns Hopkins UP, 1983), 342.

26.   Gérard Genette, *Palimpsestes*, 10.

27.   Sorela, 57.

28.   Gary Saul Morson and Caryl Emerson, ed., *Rethinking Bakhtin: Extensions and Challenges* (Evanston: Northwestern UP, 1989), 81.

29.   Gary Saul Morson and Caryl Emerson, *Rethinking Bakhtin*, 81.

30.   *Rethinking Bakhtin*, 82.

31.   The name Hofmaustall in the quote refers to Hugo von Hofmannsthal, an Austrian playwright and poet, 1874-1929.

32.   Gabriel García Márquez and Plinio Apuleyo Mendoza, *The Fragrance of Guava*, trans. Ann Wright (London: Verso, 1983), 25.

33.   *Palimpsestes*, 8.

34.   Ramón Gómez de la Serna, a Spanish writer (1888-1963), created the greguería, a short, pithy and paradoxical sentence.

35.   Sorela, 56.

36.   Sorela, 31.

37.   See Gerald Prince, *A Dictionary of Narratology* , 53.

38.   Lucien Dällenbach, "Intertexte et autotexte," *Poétique* 27 (1976), 284.   Translation is mine.   Diegesis refers to the first narrative and metadiegesis designates a narrative that is embedded in the first narrative.

Chapter 3

Journalistic Peregrinations II:
Moving Up the Coast: Barranquilla, *El Heraldo*, La Jirafa and the Hypertextual Explosion, 1950-1952

The second stage of García Márquez's journalistic career centers on his work for *El Heraldo* of Barranquilla: "The fact is that his actual debut as a regular member of the *El Heraldo* staff took place on January 5, 1950, with the first piece in his column 'La Jirafa,' which he always signed with the pseudonym of Septimus, the first of an extensive and in many ways admirable series of some four hundred columns."[1] García Márquez's writing thus undergoes a significant expansion in Barranquilla. The thirty-eight signed texts of the "Another Story" column of *El Universal* increase to nearly four hundred pieces in the "La Jirafa" column of *El Heraldo*. His literary production consists of seven short stories, a series of "notes" for a projected novel entitled *The House* and his first novel, *Leaf Storm*, which he wrote between June or July, 1950 and June, 1951. The key factors in this sudden change in his writing are personal and professional. The journalistic parameters remained intact, since he continued to work in the same open/restricted space of the column. Nothing indicates that the young writer suddenly acquired more experience and training in journalism beyond what he had gained working for *El Universal*. Nevertheless, the "La Jirafa" column differs from his first assignment because García Márquez considered "La Jirafa" as a veritable alchemical laboratory in which he could experiment more freely with his bigeneric writing.

In television the Spanish word "jirafa" refers to the "boom" or "a long movable stand, crane, arm, or pole for mounting and moving a microphone or camera."[2] This definition clearly corresponds to the task undertaken by García Márquez to extend the reach of his writing. Moreover, the use of the pseudonym *Septimus* and titles suggests an increasing personalization of the space of the column and indicate a heightened awareness of his audience. The newspaper may have required him to headline his columns because, as one of García Márquez's friends recalls, he would watch him "writing his column with surprising speed, choosing telegrams, and immediately return to his favorite haunts in the city. He would come back to the paper, write his headlines and, once again, go back to meet his friends."[3] The titles of the jirafas, whether formally required or not, open the way to the paratextual level. Like his first column, García Márquez would periodically have to draw on his personal material when he lacked a definite topic. He describes this dilemma in a piece entitled, "A Theme for a Theme," (April 11, 1950): "There are people who turn the lack of a topic into a subject for a newspaper column. The solution is absurd in a world like ours where so many incredible things are happening."[4] He adds that "journalism is the profession which most closely resembles boxing, with the advantage that the typewriter always wins, and the disadvantage that you can never throw in the towel. We will be left with a jirafa" (250). At that moment, journalism and literature were vying for domination, and he was writing in both genres as if he were under the constant pressure of time.

Another significant influence on García Márquez's writing is the "Group of Barranquilla" which included his friends Alfonso Fuenmayor, Germán Vargas and Alvaro Cepeda Samudio. The journalist Próspero Morales Pradilla coined the name of this group in his column, "Próspero's Outlook" ("El Mirador de Próspero"), in *El Espectador*.[5] However, as Germán Vargas stresses, the gatherings never constituted a literary coterie: "What Próspero Morales Pradilla called, some months later, 'the Group of Barranquilla,' began to take shape about ten years ago around the writer Ramón Vinyes, without any formal planning, without regular meetings, without any idea in mind of setting up a group. 'The Group of Barranquilla' is primarily a group of people who have been friends for many years. In no way does it constitute a 'movement,' nor what others ambitiously and mistakenly call their group, 'a generation.'"[6] The informal gatherings of the Group of Barranquilla, which now belong to the literary life and legend of García Márquez, opened new literary vistas by bringing him into contact with writers like William Faulkner, Ernest Hemingway and

Virginia Woolf. If the Group of Barranquilla succeeded in stimulating his literary interests and enabled him to envision his future writing projects, his work for *El Heraldo* required him to produce something everyday: "In Barranquilla I had to write a lot. In the course of a day I would have to write a jirafa and sometimes an editorial in addition to other anonymous pieces. This would sometimes create problems for me. Everything depended on finding the topic: once I had the subject in mind I would sit down at the typewriter and dash off my jirafa in one fell swoop."[7] Consequently, García Márquez's writing was leading an active, double life in Barranquilla.

García Márquez also engaged in two brief editorial ventures involving the magazine *Crónica* and the mininewspaper *Comprimido*. The first issue of *Crónica* appeared on April 29, 1950, and "with little financial backing and few prospects for success, [the magazine] tried to inform readers about sports and literature while maintaining, above all, high standards of journalism."[8] As editor in chief, García Márquez, along with Alfonso Fuenmayor, assumed full responsibility for the magazine. The last issue came out in June of 1951. Later that year the newspaper *Comprimido* was set up. It "was a free newspaper that pinned its continued survival on what it published and it offered readers the convenient format of highly condensed current news."[9] These two activities not only illustrate the interrelationship of the two genres in García Márquez's work, but also represent extensions of his basic writing pattern in which journalism and literature enjoy equal status. At that time, his journalistic writing not only meant earning a living, but also represented a genre worthy of serious attention. García Márquez's boisterous life in Barranquilla encouraged the development of the hybridized, bigeneric writing that dominates his later work.

In this phase, literature and journalism interface more closely, and the number and variety of texts expand dramatically. This situation precludes establishing a single critical focus, or studying the jirafas in chronological order. Consequently, this chapter concentrates on eighteen pieces which give the reader a global perspective of this period. The jirafas are divided into specific thematic categories: 1) personal themes (eight texts); 2) literary commentary (four jirafas); 3) politics and violence (four texts); and 4) Colombian culture (two texts).   Besides this thematic classification, Genette's transtextual categories serve as the principal critical focus. Paratextuality will be discussed in certain instances. In the jirafas with personal themes, hypertextuality plays the most important role. The literary columns combine hypertextuality, metatextuality and intertextuality.   Inter- and hypertextual relations dominate the political jirafas. The two cultural jirafas primarily involve inter- and autotextuality.

Narratology and Bakhtin's concepts (principally heteroglossia, dialogism and the carnivalesque), elucidate certain aspects linked to the textual and transtextual levels. Bakhtin's concepts have passed through a veritable critical gauntlet, and this situation has created confusion and ambiguity. In general, studies on Bakhtin have limited themselves to a purely literary and textual focus. While this is a perfectly legitimate area of study, Bakhtin's rich and often contradictory writings deal with a much broader context which extends far beyond strictly textual boundaries.

The concept of metalinguistics proposed by Bakhtin (and which Todorov has rechristened translinguistics), includes theoretical migrations and dialogical leakages, and gives the word *text* a much broader definition. Although Bakhtin's writings contain many contradictory and conflicting elements, this fundamental trait underpins his work from the outset and insures its constant vitality. Since his writings engender a multiplicity of critical perspectives, any application of his ideas must take into account the inevitably inherent contradictions.   Finally, this analysis discusses the elements which relate to the formal criteria of journalism (headlines, subheadings, openings, endings and style), because the column format and the journalistic environment still require adherence to certain general rules.

Unlike Hemingway, who worked for the *Kansas City Star* and wrote articles in accordance with the strict rules of a style manual, the "La Jirafa" column offered García Márquez more stylistic and thematic latitude. This lack of explicit rules and standards harmonized with the open, costeño ambience. Censorship, although less absolute on the coast than in the interior, and constantly attenuated and altered by the permanent presence of mamagallismo, still imposed certain limitations on the printed word, whatever its source and form. The increasingly repressive censorship helped set the stage for the inevitable clash between the authoritarian monoglossia of the existing political power and the open heteroglossia of costeño culture.

The above discussion does not signify that García Márquez primarily wrote his jirafas to oppose and subvert censorship, nor much less to overthrow the government. This picture of the existing sociopolitical climate shows that every text is situated and produced in specific historical and social circumstances. This relation between the text and its social context demonstrates that the textuality of the text, the text of textuality, or textology, must *necessarily* include con-texts and co-texts (transtextual relations) which contribute to the configuration of text under study. The "texts" of García Márquez, whether literary or journalistic, offer critics a unique and perhaps deceptive analytical opportunity. Within García Márquez's extensive textual network, arbitrarily divided into stable genres like journalism, novel and short story, there are "major" and "minor" texts; that is, those which he wrote to beguile his readers, and those which really enable us to understand the evolution of his bigeneric writing. The García Márquez of the early period most likely did not think of literature and journalism as distinct genres, that is, as stable categories defined by formal criteria; rather he considered journalism and literature as genres susceptible to dialogic leakages and interactions (in Bakhtinian terms), as sociopolitical genres that the spoken/written/printed word could not organize and finalize. Like Bakhtin, for whom the idea of the novel as a genre is ultimately inconceivable, García Márquez also exhibited the same flexible and pragmatic attitude towards the idea of genres.

Jirafas, Titles and Paratextuality

Although García Márquez apparently did not devote considerable time to the titles of his jirafas, they nevertheless belong to the opening which he considers so important. In the personal theme jirafas, García Márquez uses inferred headlines (a kind of headlining which interprets one or several news items) more than direct headlines (a summary of the news item).[10] The titles of these jirafas condense the news content and capture the reader's attention, while the column expands the title. These titles thus set in motion a series of resonances which the text takes up again and elaborates. Finally, the titles closely relate to the first sentence.

In "Theme for a Theme" (April 11, 1950), the opening reformulates the title and exposes it to successive transformations: "There are people who convert the lack of a subject into a topic for a news column" (249). The title constitutes an absence which demands to be filled. In "On the End of the World" (February 14, 1950), the first sentence concentrates the title in the person of Nostradamus: "You see, Septimus, Nostradamus is not such a charlatan as some people claim" (172). In "A Chat" (June 2, 1950), the column reproduces in one long sentence the title which, as an absence, calls for completion. In "Reasons for Being a Dog" (March 20, 1950), the hermeneutic function of the title resides in the word "Reasons" which poses an enigma that the reader will have to decipher, and the opening only deepens the mystery: "Someday, if I ever grew tired of this daily pounding away at the public's patience, and if I were given the right to be something entirely different, and I did not have any human limitations---not even natural ones---the exercising of that right, I would become the robust dog, bursting with health, who wanders about the business district of the city and has his comfortable and customary place in the 'Happy' Café" (220). The title of this jirafa, unlike the preceding ones, contains a hermeneutic code which presents an enigma. Therefore, it does not correspond to the two types of journalistic titles defined above (inferred and direct), because it neither informs nor interprets; on the contrary, the title poses the question---What reasons?---and the text contextualizes this question. The first sentence presents a series of hypothetical conditions which expand the enigma of the title before solving it.

In "Adam's Other Daughter" (April 4, 1950), while the title summarizes the jirafa, it presents an enigma which the first sentence really does not clarify. A certain Doctor Guido Kirch, who has been studying an ancient manuscript for ten years, discovers that "Adam and Eve had a daughter named Noaba" (242). As Alvaro Pineda Botero explains, "the relationships between the title and the text can take different forms: close, accidental or far removed."[11] In this jirafa, the ludic relation allows the author to establish a hypertextual link with the hypotext of the Bible. This title reveals two other aspects: the arbitrariness of the sign and the concealment of the truth. The title can have different meanings, and "the reader receives a multitude of 'half-truths,' truths simultaneously specified and avoided which compel the reader to continue reading, for the text conceals and does not reveal."[12] In this jirafa, Adam's other daughter is a half-truth, and the reader must be skeptical about a title which conceals more than it reveals.

The jirafa entitled "The Olfactory Inferno" (September 7, 1950) contains an inferred title because it interprets the column's content, and the opening ("The sense of smell is implacable in the individualization of memories," 433) strengthens the infernal atmosphere of the title. In "The Mystery of the Pianola" (April 21, 1951), the arbitrariness of the sign emerges as the reader begins to understand the enigma proposed by the title. The word "mystery" suggests a problem that is going to be resolved, but, since the title can contain multiple meanings, the mystery to which it refers will resurface in the jirafa. The opening sentence carries out this task: "I don't believe that Ramón has said this: 'The pianola is the only instrument which ghosts can play'" (638). The opening reinstates the sense of mystery in which the author will continue to envelop the pianola.

In another jirafa of October 21, 1952, "The Trains Turned Into Cities," García Márquez uses an inferred title which reflects his attitude about trains and their transformation into refined products of modern technology. The first sentence contradicts the title and contextualizes the reality within which he wishes to discuss trains: "When one of our country dwellers saw the train for the first time, she gave the exact definition: 'It's a kitchen carrying a town'" (839). This definition closely corresponds to the reality that García Márquez was living and writing about at that time.   This imaginative definition is deeply rooted in the costeño culture of which magical realism is an integral, daily component. It is not a literary invention but a way of seeing and experiencing reality, and this cultural code will necessarily infuse his works which are products of this milieu.   Indeed, his journalistic-literary work continues to draw its primary inspiration from this source until the publication of *The Autumn of the Patriarch* in 1975. In this novel, García Márquez initiates a phase in which exhaustive research and documentation take precedence over magical realism.[13] Therefore, the title of this last jirafa reveals an important cultural code related to his costeño vision. The verb "turned into" (se volvieron in Spanish) implies a rapid change and creates a void between "The trains" and "cities," and it sets up a binary opposition between the magical and the modern.

Obviously, the title can contain many possible meanings which the text can explore. In these jirafas, the hypotexts include the comics, the newspaper, the prophetic writings of Nostradamus, a literary text, the teletype, costeño culture, and Mark Twain. The hypertextual relations which the jirafas establish with the hypotexts can be explicit or implicit; that is, a jirafa can "speak" about, quote or "refer" to a given hypotext or can omit any mention of it. However, as Genette points out, text B (the hypertext) "could not exist as such without A (the hypotext), from which I derive the name of a process that I would still provisionally term transformation, which text B addresses in a more or less clear manner without necessarily mentioning or quoting it.[14]

Personal Theme Jirafas and Hypertextual Relations

In "Theme for a Theme," the hypotext is the same newspaper: "Whoever attempts to sit down and write about nothing, all he would have to do is glance through that day's newspaper to see his initial problem change into an entirely different one: knowing which topic he prefers among the many available to him" (249). In "On the End of the World," the title already suggests the hypotext (the prophecies of Nostradamus) to which García Márquez alludes in the jirafa: "In those disconcerting and complex prophecies---written in old French---which we talked about several weeks ago, the terrifying medieval sage says that the world will come to an end when the last descendant of Louis XVI sits on the pontifical throne" (172). The jirafa to which the author refers is "The bathtub for the Troglodyte" (January 19, 1950) in which he compares Dr. Slichter, an economics professor from Harvard, "to the enigmatic and cabalistic poet Nostradamus who took upon himself the incredible task of making sweeping prophecies in verse which were composed in such a state of confusion that only after the events have taken place can the accuracy of his predictions be known" (155).

Since hypertextual relations present a complex series of relations and permutations, it is important to specify the particular relation involved. All the hypertexts take the form of transformations and/or imitations of previous works, and their hypotexts can be explicit or implicit. In "On the End of the World," the hypertextual nexus with the previous jirafa is a supplement, which Genette defines as "a transposition in the form of continuity."[15] If in the jirafa-hypotext the author uses Nostradamus to metaparody the professor's predictions ("On the other hand, the Nostradamus of Harvard fixes dates and talks clearly and emphatically about cars and vacation trips," 155), in the following jirafa, a change in values, or transvaluation, takes place in the writings of Nostradamus. Instead of mocking these predictions, the author re-establishes the biblical role of the prophet as God's spokesperson.

The jirafa represents a supplement because it continues the tradition of Nostradamus while transposing the biblical prophet into a modern one. Another transposition from one jirafa to the other is transvocalization, the passage from the third to the second person, and the author addresses the reader in the guise of Septimus. Yet another change introduced in the second jirafa is transmotivation, or the substitution of one motive for another.[16] If the motivation in the first jirafa is to establish a kind of parodying double of the Harvard professor, the motive of a legitimate prophet replaces it in the second jirafa. The author insists that the latter jirafa "is devoted to considering in all seriousness the many events which are already announcing the imminent end of this world in which there once was a paradise" (172). Transvocalization enables the author to modernize the prophecies of Nostradamus and bring them into the present. By modernizing Nostradamus another change occurs between the hypotext and the hypertext; that is, what Genette calls transvaluation: "The valuation of a character consists of attributing, through a pragmatic or psychological transformation, a more important and/or 'sympathetic' role to him in the system of values of the hypertext which the hypotext did not grant him."[17]

The author relativizes and revitalizes the mysterious figure of Nostradamus in the hypertext, whereas in the context of costeño humor, he offers the reader a series of false prophets and prophecies which metaparody/criticize/reveal the barbarity of the modern age. President Truman, "after drinking a glass of water, gave the order to make hydrogen bombs" (172). A seventeen year old Filipino prophet "predicted that the end of the world would be confirmed last January 22" (172-73). The valuation of Nostradamus stems from the fact that his prophecies appear apocalyptic and unfinalized, and finality and the finalization of the world depend on man: "Very simply, what is happening is that humanity already has the presentiment that at some point the Day of Judgment must come from somewhere as the only solution to all the problems which are making it lose its mind" (173). The transpositions and bonds between hypotext and hypertext are multiple and rather complex, even in these short pieces. Moreover, this analysis shows the extent to which texts can interconnect and surpass the spatial limits imposed by the column without violating the formal criteria of journalism.

In "A Chat," the hypotext is the title and the jirafa constitutes the hypertext. The hypertextual transposition which the author carries out is what Genette calls transtylization, that is, "a stylistic rewriting, a transposition whose sole function is a change of style."[18] It is also necessary to take into account the related concepts of *reduction* and *augmentation* of the text. This jirafa employs augmentation and, among the subcategories established by Genette, *expansion*, which involves "doubling or tripling the reach of each sentence of the hypotext."[19] In fact, the entire jirafa is one long sentence which, in its twisting and circular course, advances through a series of continuous vacillations: If one Thursday, if ten o'clock has passed, and if, moreover, etc. The final sentence returns to the beginning with one final hesitation: "And if the page ends and there is an editor in chief standing at our side waiting; and if all that happens---in a single day---what more can a poor mortal do than write a speech even though the following day they send you somewhere else with your jirafa?" (338).

In "Reasons for Being a Dog," the hypotext offers a mixture of the meetings of the "Group of Barranquilla," the personal life of García Márquez and the consteño cultural code, of which one of the principal features is a permanent sense of humor in dealing with life and the cachaco solemnity of the interior of Colombia. This attitude also includes the carnivalization of the reality of the official world, from which the dehierarchization and inversion of the human and canine worlds derive. The carnivalization of reality starts with an imaginary inversion in which the author is going to transform himself into a dog to walk around the city. The author affirms that if he were granted the right to be something completely different, he would become "that plump dog, radiating with good health, who wanders about the commercial district of the city and has its accustomed and comfortable place to sleep in the 'Happy' Café" (220). Given the reference to the 'Happy' Café in which the members of the Group of Barranquilla would meet, the hypotext is most likely García Márquez's personal life at that time. The author uses a parody which "modifies the theme *without modifying the style.*"[20]

The author completes the transformation by utilizing an inverted logic that induces him to conclude that "it is even possible that it was the dog who domesticated man" (220). As he carries out the successive decrowning of man and the crowning of the dog, the author opens the way for the metaparody of various cultural components---politics, literature and social pretensions: "We thus find vagabond dogs---like vagabond men---who lie down to sleep in any place, without worrying about whether or not the next day their daily bone will come to them as if out of the blue" (221). In this dehierarchized world the dogs are grouped in a completely heterogeneous manner, and from this canine confusion arises the best dog, the philosophical dog, "who sleeps all day, legs stretched out, in the doorway of the 'Happy' Café (221). This jirafa-hypertext is doubly interesting because it transforms the hypotext (the personal life of the author) and metaparodies the hypotext of the social order. The strong dose of the ludic element contributes to the miniaturized creation of the costeño ambience in which the author was living.

In "Adam's Other Daughter," the news cable serves as hypo-pretext to reach the Bible, which represents one of the most ubiquitous hypotexts in García Márquez's work. García Márquez would sometimes use cabletext news items when he needed a topic for his column. As Pedro Sorela explains, "García Márquez was particularly well situated because in his position, not only as a columnist, but as 'copy editor,' he had to sort through all the news items from the international news services and decide what to publish and then headline it."[21] García Márquez deliberately distorts the news from the teletype by altering the lead which serves "to answer the questions what, who, how, when, where and why, according to the traditional norms of objective journalism."[22] In the jirafa the teletype news item from New York says that one Doctor Guido Kirch "after studying a nine hundred year old manuscript for ten years, has discovered that Adam and Eve had a daughter named Noaba" (242). This opening answers the questions *what* (the discovery of another daughter), *who* (Dr. Kirch), *how* (studying a manuscript), *when* and *where* (a cable dated New York), but it omits the *why*. The author not only leaves the motive unresolved but also negates it in the following sentence: "In reality, the Old Testament does not say anything about her" (242).

In this encounter with the most sacred hypotext in the Western World the author creates a hypertext which represents a parody and a satirical pastiche, a kind of thematic-stylistic mimetext of the Bible. Given his proverbial costeño sense of humor, what really intrigues him "is to find out why the diligent Dr. Kirch has seemingly lost all semblance of reason by spending ten years deciphering a wretched hieroglyph, only to discover a new and insignificant person in a house where they no longer physically fit. Because if one thing is certain, it is that in no other place are there so many people, real or imagined, as in the Bible" (243). This irreverence with regard to the Bible becomes a permanent part of García Márquez's work and it manifests itself on many supposedly solemn occasions.[23] This attitude helps create a hypertext in which three satirical elements contained in the term *parody* combine: strict parody, transvestitism and caricature imitation. The author creates a strict parody of the erudite text of Dr. Kirch by multiplying the number of people until it becomes impossible to decipher the biblical genealogy. This familial pullulation mocks the ardent efforts by scholars who persist in discovering something which perhaps does not exist. Concurrently, the author satirically transvestitizes the biblical genealogy by recounting the various dramatic moments in the lives of the biblical characters. Finally, he imitates the biblical style based on rhythmic repetitions: "There was a Lot whose own daughters made him sleep off the most envious hangover that one could imagine, only to complicate the whole family lineage and not to know in the end why their own children were later their own brothers and were logically grandchildren of their own father" (243). The jirafa undergoes a series of transformations which, once they are filtered through costeño mamagallismo, emerge as metaparodies which prevent the text from closing. The author's irreverence resurfaces when he asks: "Is it right for an intelligent person like Dr. Kirch to waste ten years of his precious life, only to discover an obscure daughter of Adam and Eve who possibly did not even have the admirable nutritional knowledge of her own parents?" (243-44). His answer is pure mamagallismo: "Ten years is a lot of time in the life of a man to waste it on a single daughter" (244). In this jirafa, like many others, García Márquez combines elements from the immense hypotext of costeño culture in order to create hypertexts that extend and link the components of his Infinite Text that he will continue to write under different titles.

The hypotext-costeño culture/hypertext-journalistic-literary work relation will expand and deepen as García Márquez continues to perfect his bigeneric writing. Genette compares hypertextuality to the concept of *bricolage* which Claude Lévi-Strauss uses to characterize the thinking process of the "savage" mind of people who belong to so-called "primitive" or "prescientific" societies.[24] Genette affirms that "the art of 'creating something new from something old' offers the advantage of producing more complex and pleasing objects than products which are 'made-to-order': a new function is superimposed and combines with the old structure, and the dissonance between these two copresent elements gives the whole its distinctive flavor. This object duality, in the order of textual relations, can be envisioned in the old image of the *palimpsest*. On the same parchment, one text can be seen superimposed on another in such a manner that the old text is still visible to the eye."[25] In the same manner, this and many other jirafas function as palimpsests in which the hypo-hypertextual relationship shows through and García Márquez's evolving writing produces the new from the old. As Genette says, the importance of hypertextuality resides in the fact that "the Borgesian utopia of a literature in perpetual transfusion (or transtextual perfusion) is thus realized, constantly present to itself in its totality and as a Totality, of which all the authors combine into one, and of which all the books are one vast Book, a single Infinite Book."[26]

The costeño hypotext reappears in "The Olfactory Inferno," in the panoply of rich smells which its openness and street culture generate. This jirafa constitutes a veritable text-program of Baudelairian synesthesia in which "one type of stimulation evokes the sensation of another, as the hearing of a sound resulting in the sensation of the visualization of a color."[27] The author describes the sense of smell as "an instrument of torture, a kind of private inferno which will always systematically recall to us all the objects into which we have for better or worse introduced our noses" (432). The immediate reaction is to consider this jirafa, like many of the texts which precede *OHYS*, as an insignificant hypotext or, even worse, as an insignificant pre-text, a juvenile exercise. This jirafa relates to another hypotext which is rooted either in the author's childhood or in the costeño ambience. Although the hypertext may not mention the hypotext, it could not exist without it.

This jirafa most likely gathers up the smells of the costeño cultural milieu, transforms them into words, and creates a text that the author literally hopes the reader will be able to smell. But how can the reader possibly detect the "smell" of a text? The author succeeds in making the reader experience the olfactory dimension of the jirafa through a synesthetic defamiliarization of reality which requires him to recontextualize the smell. The sense of smell, indissolubly linked to memory, constitutes a hypotext which the author progressively incorporates into his writing until it reaches its fullest expression in *OHYS*. When critics mention García Márquez's "cultural demons," they are usually referring to Ernest Hemingway and William Faulkner. Nevertheless, in this jirafa, it seems valid to include other cultural demons; that is, the "French connection," including Marcel Proust and possibly Gustave Flaubert. The author says that "the sense of smell is implacable in the individualization of memories" (433). The effects of different smells on people in this jirafa represent a veritable "Proustitution" of this olfactory sense. The eucalyptus smell "is not merely the memory of the tree. It is moreover the sky, with its color, somber with its sad horizon; and it persists longer than the last view of the tree and the sky. Suddenly the smell is filled with houses, people who are walking, and whom we see from behind because the vagueness of the memory does not permit us to make out the faces" (433). Like the famous Proustian scene of the madeleine in which its taste spontaneously opens the door to the narrator's childhood in Combray, the eucalyptus fragrance evokes and restores the past in its quasi-totality.

This jirafa also deprivileges the sense of sight which dominates the work of Hemingway. Smell invades and penetrates everything and engraves itself in memory. A woman used a bitter perfume "which forever remained embedded in her memory, like the picture of a smell" (433). The synesthetic link is established between a bitter perfume and the picture of a smell. The author says that "an entire day is nothing but a vague succession of smells" (433), so that smell becomes time, another synesthetic combination. Smells in García Márquez do not function in the same way as in Proust because no clear distinction is drawn between voluntary memory (the memory of routine) and involuntary memory (spontaneous and fragile memory). In García Márquez, the hypotext of costeño culture furnishes him with a wide variety of smells associated with memories. In many instances, memories represent the only patrimony of the innumerable forgotten towns of Latin America which have suffered the dire consequences of economic booms. In García Márquez's costeño region, it was the banana fever that passed through these towns like a whirlwind, creating a rapid and illusory prosperity that disappeared as swiftly as it had appeared, leaving these towns buried and paralyzed in their bitter nostalgia. Smells form an integral part of this region. Beyond describing the atmosphere of these towns in other jirafas, the author gives one element taken from this hypotext: "Because I once met a simpleton who was very happy living by eating just arepa (a round maize loaf), since when he ate it he would remember a smell of stewed meat that he once smelled" (433). The author concludes the jirafa with another synesthetic combination: "J. R. J. would ask: 'What does love smell like?' The answer could be: 'It smells green'" (433). Green love joins two different senses---smell and sight---and shows the extent to which the cultural hypotext represents a rich source of raw material that the successive hypertexts will continue to transform in original and surprising ways.

"The Mystery of the Pianola" offers a two-fold hypotext---costeño culture and perhaps the work of Mark Twain---because the paddle steamers made regular trips up and down the Magdalena and Mississippi Rivers. Although the paddle steamer reappears in several later novels (*OHYS, Chronicle of a Death Foretold, Love in the Time of Cholera* and *The General in his Labyrinth*), in this jirafa, the pianola occupies center stage. The pianola does not exist within costeño culture, and the author draws on a fictional hypotext to create and assimilate the pianola to his cultural hypotext: "Once I heard the story of ghost ship which on a certain day of the month would travel down the Mississippi---and the story does not come from Mark Twain, although it takes place on the Mississippi and has a ghost ship---with the lights extinguished, empty, phantasmal, with the paddle wheel turning by virtue of a supernatural force" (638). If the author refers to Mark Twain in order to naturalize his text, he refuses to attribute the story to him because he wants to detach the pianola from an extrinsic cultural context. In fact, he continues to incorporate the pianola into his jirafa-hypertext by eliminating everything except this instrument: "There could be nothing---not even a boat---but there was a pianola. An eternal, melancholic pianola, whose music kept on playing above the shipwrecks" (638). Like many ostensibly anachronistic elements in García Márquez's work, he is able to revitalize them in the context of magic realism. The jirafas are hypertextual gristmills and, in this case, "no one has ever discovered who is playing the music on the pianolas and why, by simply rewinding the roll, the invisible performer pleases the audience and performs the song in reverse" (639).

The same phenomenon appears in the jirafa "The Trains Turned Into Cities" which opens with a definition which derives from the hypotext of costeño culture: "'It is a kitchen carrying a town'" (839).[28] The first trains were enchanted entities capable of fascinating the passengers and overcoming any anachronism in order to enjoy a new existence within the costeño environment.

These objects, revitalized in the jirafa-hypertext, always closely relate to the author's central focus---the human context: "Inside it was very uncomfortable. It smelled of slack, cooked food and people. Nowhere else was the real smell of humanity better appreciated than in those trains with two long, partially filled cars in which people traveled along with the sacks of plantain, trunks and wooden crates. If the word 'democracy' had not existed long before this time, it would have been easy to invent it in a train" (840). As long as the trains preserved their human context, they could continue to thrive in the realm of magic realism. The magic quality of these trains started to disappear "the moment the intellectuals discovered that it was in good taste to travel by train. And in a certain way that is how it was until the police also discovered it" (840). If this jirafa lacks a definite theme, the author always seems to return to the costeño cultural hypotext in which objects are necessarily anachronistic because they perform functions which clash with the ideas of progress and modernity. This situation results in a temporal conflict regarding the position that the object occupies and its use within a given culture. These two jirafas do not represent mere exercises in nostalgia but rather a solid vindication of the costeño hypotext as a cornucopia of elements that can contribute to the shaping of a totalizing and universal vision.

The paucity of topics in these personal jirafas enables the author to draw on his own cultural hypotext without adhering to strict standards that governed Hemingway's work as a journalist. These formal lacunas open the way to the creation of a series of hypertextual relations based almost exclusively on the hypotext of costeño culture and on the permanent sense of humor towards life. If we still have not examined the orthodox standards of journalism, it is because these jirafas are hybrid, embryonic texts with regard to their generic classification. These jirafas may be written in the column format, but evidently they do not correspond to the standard definition of the newspaper column.

Literary Jirafas and Paratextual, Metatextual and Intertextual Relations

If it is difficult to define the bigeneric quality of the previous jirafas, the literary pieces complexify the issue even further.[29] In general, the columnist comments on local, national and international news, sports or social events in a fixed space in the newspaper, and he becomes identified with a certain type of column. His readers also must remain rather well-defined to insure the success of the column. Nevertheless, it would be inaccurate to consider the García Márquez of this period an innocuous novice in journalism since the open format of the column contributed to the development of his bigeneric writing. Despite this situation, he was writing a column in a newspaper which adhered to general professional standards and which had to comply with the growing restrictions imposed by the stifling censorship. Therefore, to judge his column solely according to orthodox journalistic criteria would automatically exclude too many essential elements. Moreover, the thematic variety of the column does not violate journalistic standards because the newspaper did not assign him a specific topic for the column.

These jirafas raise the problem of the particular audience to which they are addressed. For example, how many readers were acquainted with the work of Kafka or Faulkner? The author seems to violate the journalistic norms because he targets a special audience---his friends in the Group of Barranquilla---and not the "man in the street," that is, the average reader. If he headlines his columns to capture the attention of the reader, the titles of these literary jirafas do not achieve this goal. "Caricature of Kafka" is not a title but a microtext that the jirafa converts into a mimetext by expanding it. In "Faulkner, Nobel Prize Winner," the ostensibly direct title that summarizes the jirafa reveals more about the personal preferences of the author. These titles also are microtexts which he will expand in the literary jirafas. In "Faulkner, Nobel Prize Winner," the author binarizes the writer and the prize. The most exclusive title is "Self-Critique." Besides presenting the content of the jirafa in embryonic form, it announces that the commentary will ultimately be addressed to the author himself. These titles also lack definite articles. It is not "The Caricature of Kafka" so that the title forms a syntagm or a unified concept. The title "Faulkner, Nobel Prize Winner" lacks one element (William) which would balance and officialize the title in accordance with the gravity of the honor bestowed on him.

The titles "Faulkner, Nobel Prize Winner" and "The Article on Faulkner" show the arbitrariness of the sign because they conceal more than they reveal. In "Faulkner, Nobel Prize Winner," the reader could reasonably expect the author to emphasize the ceremony and the great honor represented by the Nobel Prize, but the jirafa concentrates on Faulkner the writer. In "The Article on Faulkner," the title frames the text, but the real "article" is an imaginary one which García Márquez writes about Faulkner in the jirafa. In "Self-Critique," the title again conceals more than it reveals, especially considering that the basic function of the journalistic headline is to kernelize the news for the reader and impact him from the outset. García Márquez's titles only deliver "half-truths" to the readers because the jirafas reinterpret the meaning of the titles.

Several important points emerge from this discussion of titles. First, the act of headlining his jirafas represents a small but significant step in the journalism of the author. Besides indicating the bigeneric relationship, these titles, like the jirafas, reflect the circumstances in which the young writer was working: Neither his journalism nor his fiction of the period afforded him a well-defined context for his writing. This absence of a solid context worked to the young writer's advantage because it promoted the bigeneric expression of his writing. These titles do not fulfill journalistic criteria because they are intended for a particular audience (and in more than one case the audience could have been the author himself). These titles are more literary because they create expectation in the reader and keep him in suspense until the end of the jirafa.

In "Caricature of Kafka" (August 23, 1950), the hypotexts are the work of the Kafka and the first short stories of García Márquez. According to García Márquez, "it was through Kafka, who recounted things in German the same way my grandmother used to. When I read *Metamorphosis*, at seventeen, I realized I could be a writer."[30] Kafka undoubtedly turned into one of the cultural demons of the young writer, and his first short stories reflect a strong Kafkaesque influence. Indeed, they exhibit an excessive thematic and stylistic imitation that results in texts completely disconnected from the author's personal experience. Underlying this jirafa is the tacit presence of censorship, and the young author, in search of topics, prefers those which do not come under such close scrutiny. Moreover, it is possible that García Márquez is beginning to realize that he has exhausted the literary possibilities of Kafka, that he can carnivalize this cultural demon without losing contact with his literary work, and that he can overcome the morbidity, abstraction and the imitative style of Kafka so prevalent in his first stories.

This jirafa constitutes a parody of Kafka and, by extension, of the stories of García Márquez, and a satiric pastiche of Kafka and his own stories. García Márquez had already published various "Notes for a Novel" for an unfinished novel called *The House* and a short story, "The Woman Who Came at Six O'Clock" (June 24, 1950), which showed the influence of Hemingway. In "Caricature of Kafka," the author creates a heavy, onerous atmosphere instead of internalizing these same feelings. The jirafa opens *in media res*: "It was daybreak when F...reached the bridge" (415). The whole episode is suspended until the last sentence when the guard throws F... over the side of the bridge: "While F... was falling, he managed to see the guard carefully shaking his webbed hands" (417). The parody of the Kafka hypotext (most likely *The Trial*) changes the first letter of the name of K to F, which suggests the name of Franz. Moreover, F...'s principal problem, trying to decide how to cross the bridge, parodies the profoundly absurd situation which K... faces in *The Trial*: "He could not decide between the only four possible ways: walking briskly on the wooden planks, trotting, keeping one's balance by holding on to the handrail or jumping from wire to wire, like the circus acrobats who in a flash jump from trapeze to trapeze above the frightened crowd" (416). F... keeps on vacillating until the fifth day when, driven by hunger and thirst, he tries to say hello to a man whom he thinks is standing guard. The man, who is wearing a uniform smelling of liquor and drugs, picks him up and throws him into the water. The reference to the "webbed hands" is the only element of surprise, and it caricatures Kafka's *Metamorphosis*.

The author also creates a satiric pastiche of the Kafka-short stories hypotext. Facing the bridge, F... "raised his eyes, and through the mist he saw the powerful metallic, arc-shaped structure which stretched across the dark and turbulent waters" (415). This jirafa intertextualizes with *The Trial* and *The Metamorphosis* in an eidetic (the webbed hands) and diegetic (the absurd situation of F...) manner, and the hypertext transforms them into parody and pastiche. Beyond the direct parody of Kafka looms the metaparody of García Márquez's short stories in which his characters-states also find themselves in static situations where they are unable to decide or act. Therefore, this jirafa parodies, metaparodies and finishes by parodying itself because it deploys a series of hypertextual transformations which are not finalized.

In the two jirafas on William Faulkner, "Faulkner, Nobel Prize Winner" (November 13, 1950) and "The Article on Faulkner" (January 15, 1950), the author sets up a hypertextual relation that he will keep on expanding in his fiction: the extraordinary work and person of the southern writer William Faulkner. The Faulknerian hypotext probably arose from his readings and conversations with his friends in the Group of Barranquilla. This hypertextual relationship will start to appear in his literary work with the publication of his short story, "Nabo, the Black Man Who Made the Angels Wait" (March 17, 1951). His first novel, *Leaf Storm*, written in 1951 and published in 1955, also resembles Faulkner's novel, *As I Lay Dying*. The Faulknerian hypotext also differs in the strong personal identification of García Márquez with the writer and his eclectic way of writing. The author says in the first jirafa: "The master William Faulkner, in his isolated house located in Oxford,

Mississippi, must have received the news with the indifference of one who sees a latecomer arrive, and it will add nothing new to his long and patient work as a writer, but will instead impose on him the cumbersome privilege of making him popular" (494). For Faulkner, the pure writer, the two poles of his existence were solitude and glory. From the beginning, García Márquez always applies the epithet "master" to Faulkner, and it shows the importance that he attributes to this hypotext.[31] After the publication of *OHYS*, García Márquez's career will also be divided between solitude and glory.

The double affiliation of García Márquez with the Faulknerian hypotext opposes the official world of the Swedish Academy which constitutes the metatextual relation in the *jirafa*. The author contrasts the indisputable greatness of William Faulkner with the long tradition of the Nobel Prize committee of awarding the prize to authors of questionable merit: "Will there be any possible way to alleviate the uneasy feeling of disagreement that is caused by the sight of one of the most important writers of all time being put in the same category with so many others of dubious distinction?" (495). While the author's enthusiastic appraisal of Faulkner prompts him to criticize the Swedish committee a little excessively, his own literary work of the period allies itself more and more with the Faulknerian hypotext. The author's admiration for this solitary and iconoclastic writer also implicitly criticizes the prevailing censorship: "The Noble Prize for Literature has been following a path in which the master Faulkner is something of a surprising break that creates serious difficulties in the future for those in charge of awarding the coveted international prize" and "the choice of Faulkner breaks with tradition" (494-95).

The Nobel Prize, which is the highest honor that the official world can bestow on an author, is a double-edged sword. Besides paying tribute to the author's work, the Nobel Prize can censure the same work by separating it and the author from the human context and absorbing them into the official world. García Márquez warns that "in any case, the honor which has just been made public will make the master the subject of much attention" (495). The last sentence of the jirafa restores the primacy of the literary hypertext despite the official world's attempt to absorb Faulkner: "The Sartoris family will start to be seen as the symbol of a sorrowful and decadent South and the Snopes family as the seething ferment of a future forged by brute force in a free-wheeling and savage struggle with nature" (495). This jirafa attests to the inevitable conflict between centripetal and centrifugal forces, which Bakhtin calls heteroglossia, or the diversity of languages. By combining a metatextual and hypertextual relation in the jirafa between the work and life of Faulkner and the official world of the Swedish Academy, the author also unleashes a conflictive heteroglossia surrounding Faulkner.

"The Article on Faulkner" presents the other side of the Faulknerian hypotext in which the author concentrates on the person of the writer. The picture he offers to the reader coincides more with the costeño spirit than with the official, serious image of an author who has just received the Nobel Prize. Indeed, Faulkner resembles what Bakhtin calls a parodying double in which "various images (for example, carnival pairs of various sorts) parodied one another variously and from various points of view; it was like an entire system of crooked mirrors, elongating, diminishing, distorting in various directions and to various degrees."[32] García Márquez distorts an article which has already passed through various communication channels before reaching the author: "The interview granted in Paris by the master William Faulkner which we read about in the extraordinary reporting of the correspondent Juan B. Fernández R.,---published by the weekly 'Crónica,' and reprinted by this newspaper---appeared yesterday in a literary supplement in Bogotá" (563). In the jirafa-hypertext, the author makes two changes which lead to the creation of the parodying double. First, he devalues the official image of the Nobel Prize laureate. He depicts Faulkner in the "existentialist gallery of the Café Flore" where he "calmly made this declaration: 'I am not a man of letters. I am a farmer who likes to tell stories'" (563). This same writer has "seventeen published novels being read throughout the world in different languages," and his declaration, according to the author, "had to disconcert the bearded and extravagantly dressed habitués of the Café Flore" (563). The literati of the Café Flore, who take themselves so seriously, also become parodic images which help increase Faulkner's stature by opposition.

The second hypertextual transformation consists of transvaluing Faulkner through the deployment of parodying doubles. The jirafa parodies the official image of the writer by quoting Faulkner's self-parody: "I write for pleasure, like others who make cages for crickets or take a break from their work by playing the saxophone or the zither" (563). While the Faulknerian hypotext already closely aligns itself with costeño culture, the author produces a text which constantly opens up to the hypertextual possibilities with other jirafas. By quoting Faulkner's answers from the interview, the author transvocalizes the hypotext, and this enables him to authenticate the parodying double of Faulkner. Journalists also utilize transvocalization, but the author transcends the formal criteria and discards the cherished notion of journalistic objectivity. The author's great admiration for Faulkner induces him to create his own costeño Faulkner who bears little resemblance to the Nobel Prize laureate. Faulkner, the novelist, labelled as obscure and chaotic, incomprehensible and turbulent, leaves a note in his hotel room in which he describes the writer's vocation: "I believe that the younger generation has nothing to say, whence its search for the bizarre, the nebulous and the barely comprehensible. The difficult part is simplicity, but there is no trick to simplicity, and the writer discovers it right when he feels empty" (564).

Given the circular path that the interview followed before reaching García Márquez, he has probably modified it to produce a hypertext which removes Faulkner from certain contexts that do not correspond to his own vision of the Southern writer. These two jirafas intertextualize with "Caricature of Kafka" in the sense that parody plays a prominent role in the three pieces, and the hypotexts also constitute cultural demons of the young writer. The three jirafas also map out the different stages that García Márquez's hypotexts follow. In "Caricature of Kafka" the author parodies Kafka (and, by extension, himself) in order to liberate himself, whereas, in the jirafas on Faulkner, parody serves to transvalue Faulkner turned costeño. Faulkner's remarks also reveal the mamagallismo of many other jirafas. The novel and short story written by García Márquez after these jirafas corroborate the fundamental change in the literary hypotext on which he will rely to create his own journalistic-literary hypertexts.

The last literary jirafa, "Self-Critique" (March 30, 1952), relates to another hypotext-cultural demon, Ernest Hemingway, and more directly, to García Márquez's literary production. Critics generally cite two novels by García Márquez, *No One Writes to the Colonel* (1961) and *In Evil Hour* (1962), as the most conspicuous evidence of Hemingway's influence. However, thanks to the exhaustive research of Jacques Gilard, we now know that Hemingway hypotext dates back to at least 1950: "In the first months of 1950, at nearly the same time that he became involved with the Group of Barranquilla, García Márquez was reading borrowed copies of the Hemingway's novels in Spanish, published just a few years before in Buenos Aires."[33] In "Self-Critique," the conjunction between the hypotext and the hypertext takes the form of two short stories.[34] Hemingway wrote his short story "The Assassins" in the "Pensión Aguilar on San Jerónimo street in Madrid on May 16, 1926, and it was published the following year in *Scribner's Magazine*. Later, it was included in the collection of short stories by Hemingway entitled *Men Without Women*. Alfonso Fuenmayor, a friend and colleague of García Márquez in the Group of Barranquilla, published an early and close translation of the Hemingway short story in *Revista de América* in October of 1945, and republished it in *Estampa* in 1949, and also in *Crónica* in 1950---that is, the same magazine and the same year that García Márquez published his 'The Woman Who Came at Six O'Clock.'"[35]

The Hemingway hypotext has thus been interacting with other hypotexts that the jirafas have drawn on and changed into hypertexts. "Self-Critique" raises the problem of distinguishing between *previous* and *subsequent* texts, but, for that same reason, it constitutes a more interesting field of investigation. Although the jirafas represent in one sense the *raw material* of his subsequent work, these pieces cannot be regarded as insignificant *pre-texts.* Pedro Sorela underscores this point:

> In order to read the journalistic work of García Márquez it must not be forgotten---as if that were possible---that it parallels his creative work, and that, of its different forms, the writer considers the short story a superior genre. Similarly, it should be remembered---and this is a more likely possibility---that the novelist is also a journalist who has exercised this profession for thirty years with few interruptions, assuming that we were to study his "literary" work at all. Both observations would be due to the same situation: Although his literary and journalistic work differ in importance and volume---his journalistic writing is somewhat more extensive than his literary production---and if the former possesses more than enough qualities to stand on its own, it is extremely difficult to understand one without a detailed reading of the other. And if there were still skeptics, suffice it to recall the words of the writer that "in my novels there is not one line which is not based on reality." That is, the primary goal of the journalist to narrate real events is inherited by the novelist.[36]

As Sorela points out, these jirafas confirm that in this early stage the author is already "Garciamarquianizing" his raw material, that is, he is literaturizing his journalism and "journalisticizing" his literary works to dialogize and "bigenericize" his writing.

If "Self-Critique" is yet another jirafa without a definite topic, this thematic void also enables the author to create important hypertexts for his work. This jirafa corresponds to the Genettian idea of the palimpsest.[37] This jirafa also makes use of the technique of *bricolage* to make something new out of old odds and ends. In this case, the old is the Hemingway story on which García

Márquez superimposes his story, and the jirafa establishes a double meta- and hypertextual relation with the two stories. Jirafas like "Self-Critique" which do not derive from an immediately recognizable journalistic hypotext, open the way for generating hypotexts originating in costeño culture and the personal experience of the author. This open hypo-hypertextual field also enables García Márquez to re-evaluate the external literary hypotexts like Kafka and Faulkner, and to produce the caricature of Kafka and the two pieces on Faulkner. "Self-Critique" is also a product of this accessible, hypertextual domain.

In "Self-Critique" the intersection of various hypotexts and hypertexts forms an interconnected web of textual relations which continuously conflict in the evolution of the Garciamarquian Text. The short story, "The Woman Who Came at Six O'Clock," to which García Márquez refers, belongs to the hypotext of the Group of Barranquilla: "It happened that Alfonso Fuenmayor bet that I could not write a detective story. I accepted the challenge, I worked out the plot, and I decided to write it" (724). The other hypotext is, of course, Ernest Hemingway's story, "The Assassins." The author believes that his own story suffers from "the dialogues, especially the woman's words which are too stilted. The words are more intelligent than the character" (724). He alludes to the first version which contained "low class dialogues. They were much better suited to that taciturn, fallen woman who has just committed a crime for the simple reason that she is bored" (724).

Initially, García Márquez may have imitated the tense, terse, colloquial dialogue of Hemingway, but in the final version he felt obligated to polish the woman's speech, and that change resulted in the false dialogues: "The woman has become brilliant, clever, and perhaps false" (724-25). García Márquez concludes that the story "resembles Hemingway more than G. G. M." (725). This statement not only shows that the hypertextual relation with Hemingway is much less stable than that which he has established with Faulkner, but also that the author, without quoting Hemingway's story, initiates a metatextual relation with the story: "Finally, that story is a big problem. Seriously speaking, I have to tell you that I am publishing it without yet knowing for sure if it is as good as I believe, or whether I have let myself be deceived by a mirage" (725).

The Faulknerian hypotext fully emerges when the author describes his visit to his native town of Aracataca: "I have just returned from Aracataca. It is still a dusty village, filled with its old colonels fading away in the back yard, under the last banana tree, and a striking number of 60 year old virgins, decaying, sweating away the last vestiges of their sex in the two o'clock afternoon drowsiness" (725). More than a transformation, this passage represents a direct transfer of the Faulknerian vision to the jirafa-hypertext, a connection which none of the other hypotexts offers to the author. The Faulknerian hypertext overshadows the others and its importance surfaces in the García Márquez's reaction to his visit: "I had intended to write a chronicle about this trip, but now I have decided to save the material for *The House*, a big seven hundred page novel I plan to finish within two years" (726).

"Self-Critique" and the other literary pieces make up a single text and delineate the different stages of the Garciamarquian hypertextuality. In addition, the changes in his literary production and his hypotexts coincide more or less with dates of the jirafas. In "Self-Critique," the three cultural demons of García Márquez converge---Kafka, Hemingway and Faulkner---and inevitably one hypotext will dominate at any given moment. The jirafas, much more than his literary work of the period, set in motion the transtextual vibrations which will enable him to continue to develop his writing and vision. "Self-Critique" crystallizes a crucial moment in the hypertextual intersection of the author's writing. The unfinalized nature of the jirafas engenders hypertextual writing since the author, lacking definite subjects, draws on the hypotexts which originate in his own culture and experience. The immediacy and ephemerality of journalistic hypotexts require finalization and closure, and do not encourage the creation of hypertextual relations. From this standpoint, the author's lack of training in journalism and formal criteria promote the development of the Garciamarquian Text.

Political Jirafas With Intertextual and Hypertextual Relations

When we turn our attention to the political columns, we soon realize that García Márquez subjects politics and violence to the same costeño humor. This approach does not deny the presence of censorship, the serious sociopolitical instability of Colombia in the 1950s, or the possible confrontation with the government: "Under the pretext of 'The Violence,' censorship was established which, while in-house in Barranquilla, was not easy to avoid completely."[38] Since political themes could pose serious problems for the young writer, he did not openly commit himself to the defense of a specific cause in his jirafas because the columns represented his only steady source of income. This does not mean that García Márquez lacked political convictions, but his political thought, like his writing, refused to align itself with a specific movement.

Indeed, the many attempts to define exactly the politics of García Márquez, not only during his costeño period but throughout his career, have produced few concrete results. He has vigorously defended and promoted different causes, he has repeatedly stated that he wants the world to be socialist, he has called himself an "emergency politician," but he has never openly embraced a single political philosophy---neither Marxist, Leninist, nor Communist. As Pedro Sorela explains:

> We must also understand that García Márquez has never been a "protest," writer, neither during his costeño period, when he had less time to write what he wanted, nor later on, when he was certainly able to do it. Even when he defended the most committed and partisan positions, he did it in a tangential literary way, and the quality of his journalistic texts is, for the most part, separate from the topic they discuss. There is no evidence that García Márquez has ever subscribed to the widely held belief that "polemic writing" has to use a more vulgar language "accessible to the masses," for the simple reason that all his work attests

to the belief that "every" piece of writing must meet that condition. And it is possible that that belief comes from journalism, since he clearly prizes clarity and simplicity as the principal qualities of all writing.[39]

The author wrote his political jirafas at the time when a conjunction of factors led to the hybridization of the jirafas. In Bakhtinian terms, hybridization is "the mixing, within a single concrete utterance, of two or more different linguistic consciousness, often widely separated in time and social space. Since hybrids can be read as belonging simultaneously to two or more systems, they cannot be isolated by formal grammatical means."[40] This double-voiced quality of hybrids relates closely to the concept of transtextuality. The restricted space of the column can also inhibit the development of a well-defined political position. García Márquez's work as an investigative reporter for *El Espectador* in Bogotá will firmly establish his opposition to the hypotext of the repressive government of Rojas Pinilla, and this position will crystallize and culminate in his fourteen part series on the accident of the destroyer *A. R. C. Caldas* known as *The Story of a Shipwrecked Sailor*. During his investigative reporting the rapid expansion of journalistic space coincides with thematic and narrative alterations in his literary output, especially the creation of a double narrator, the fictionalization of the reader, and the copresence and application of literary and journalistic techniques to his articles. Unlike the other jirafas analyzed in this chapter, the political columns are studied in chronological order to underscore the changes in his political thinking.

In "A Woman of Importance" (January 11, 1950), the hypotext is multifaceted. The center stage is occupied by the dictatorial government of Juan Domingo Perón while Franco's Fascist government looms in the background. In the case of Argentina and Perón, the military establishment had admired and imitated the German military traditions since the late 19th century, and Franco's Spain remained solidly linked to Fascism until his death in 1975. Another hypotext is the Group of Barranquilla and the influence of its spiritual leader, Ramón Vinyes: "We have to remember the strong influence that Ramón Vinyes had on García Márquez and the other members of the Group of Barranquilla. This influence was not only literary, as García Márquez himself has recognized, and his political influence was so prevalent that the young Colombian journalist acquired such a strong aversion for Franco that, like Malraux, he swore never to go to Spain as long as Franco was alive."[41]   Moreover, the constant presence of the costeño hypotext encompasses the others and necessarily influences the configuration of all the jirafas.   Finally, the jirafa obliquely criticizes the conservative government of Colombia whose censorship was becoming progressively more repressive and restrictive.

To set in motion the different textual components in this jirafa, the author uses the narrative strategy of the oppositional arrangement of perspectives which "sets norms against one another by showing up the deficiencies of each norm when viewed from the standpoint of the others."[42]   The author creates a series of contrasting norms between *governing/acting*, then proceeds to produce a highly ironic portrait of the Eva Duarte and Juan Domingo Perón.   These contrasting norms alternate and produce a parodic transformation that in turn changes into metaparody; that is, if Juan and Eva cannot *govern*, they can *act*, and if they cannot *act*, they can try to govern again.   Each parodied parody further undermines and subverts the status of the famous couple, and the parodies continue to multiply without concluding.   This type of metaparodic subversion coincides with the constant interplay and manipulation by García Márquez of the available and pre-existing hypotexts.   Even at this early stage of his career García Márquez seemed to have realized that direct confrontation with the power structure would limit him to a single hypotext. Since any hypotext always ends up binding itself to a multitude of other ones, he could not eliminate them without falsifying the reality which he wanted to explore in his writings.

After situating these political jirafas, we see the same parodic attitude being applied to the dictatorship of Juan Domingo Perón. The parody takes the form of a semiotic square, which is "the visual representation of the logical articulation of any semantic category or, in other words, the visual representation of the constitutive model describing the elementary structures of signification."[43] In the Greimassian model, "given a unit of sense S_1 (e.g., rich), it signifies in terms of relations with its contradictory $\overline{S}_1$ (not rich), its contrary S_2 (poor), and the contradictory of S_2 ($\overline{S}_2$, not poor)."[44] In Greimas's system, "the (semantic) course of a narrative can be said to correspond to a movement along the semiotic square: the narrative deploys itself in terms of operations (transformations) leading from a given unit to its contrary (or contradictory)."[45]

If we apply this concept to the jirafa "A Woman of Importance," we can represent the parody in the following diagram:

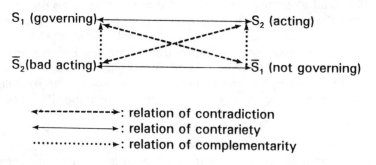

           ◂- - - - - - - - - -▸ : relation of contradiction
           ◂──────────▸ : relation of contrariety
           ··················▸ : relation of complementarity

The semiotic square shows how the narrative deploys itself in the jirafa, keeping in mind the hypotexts and the contrasting norms between *governing* and *acting*, which appear in the first sentence: "When Eva Duarte and Juan Domingo Perón put their necks in the conjugal noose, she was nothing but a vague memory of a mediocre movie" (149). The norm is the government of Perón (S_1). The first norm, *governing*, leads to its contrary, *acting* (S_2). Eva Duarte is a "second rate actress" who will play a central role in "that other big film extravaganza which is the present Argentine government" (149). The contrasting norm of *acting* (S_2) progressively displaces that of *governing* so that the Hollywood soap opera dimension becomes the dominant symbol of their rule:

"The honeymoon of Eva and Juan Domingo Perón was almost a coup d'état to the prejudices of Latin American high society and an opportunity for the newlyweds to show that their acting ability could surpass the insignificant film tragedies" (149). The expressions "honeymoon" and "coup d'état" link two norms since Perón did enjoy a political honeymoon period at the beginning of his rule, and he was elected president in 1945 after having participated in a military coup in 1943.

These same expressions, however, are ironic because Perón's government becomes identified with its complement, *bad acting* ($\overline{S}_2$), which first negates the political norm and then itself is negated: "Overnight---to use an original expression---Eva discovered that her second rate star's dressing room was replaced by a militarized executive cabinet, and that her role as an unemployed actress was becoming a dominant factor in the dangerous and sometimes ridiculous plot of the official operetta" 149). The expression "overnight" is highly ironic because it illustrates how movie stars are often created and, in the case of Eva, she became a political star in the same way. The expression also establishes the relation of contradiction between *governing* (S_1) and *not governing* ($\overline{S}_1$).

In this continuous series of negating negations, Perón's government is reduced, in contrast to ordinary marriages, to the "exciting and coveted sport of converting the awesome problems of state into simple conjugal pastimes" (149). Through a sequence of oppositional arrangement of perspectives the government of Juan Perón transforms itself into a soap opera devoid of substance. The norm *governing* (S_1) ends up being reduced to its complement *bad acting* ($\overline{S}_2$) as the narrative carries out a series of increasingly parodic transformations. The author expands the theatrical parallel within the norm *bad acting*: "Then came the second act, Eva's famous trip through Europe" (149-50). During her diplomatic whirlwind through Europe, each phase takes place within a constantly changing and comic perspective which undercuts the political pretensions of the Perón regime. In Spain, "the comic statesmen received her with the enthusiasm of magnanimous colleagues" (150). The author includes Spain in the norm *bad acting* since he was adamantly opposed to Franquismo; that is, neither Perón nor Franco can act. Since *bad acting* constitutes the principal norm of their respective governments, neither leader can *govern* (relation of complementarity), and the contrary is *acting* and the contradictory standard is *not governing*.

The author continues his parody by using the "alarming news from the teletype" which describes Eva's famous illness: "Eva is a woman who is so sure of herself and with such a well-defined personality that she has suffered an attack of appendicitis in public without feeling the least bit guilty" (150). The author returns to the first norm, *governing*, to metaparody the norm of *bad acting* because Eva's appendicitis "must have already been transformed into a kind of national disease, with compulsory obedience for all Argentine citizens, guaranteed by means of an executive decree" (150). The author appropriates the official government discourse which naturally depicts Eva and Perón in hyperbolically positive terms and interweaves it with discourses originating outside Argentina. In official terms, even after her operation, "Eva will emerge from it looking more beautiful as she draws ever closer to a state of ideal simplicity" (150). This internal perspective is then undercut by an external one in which Eva, with or without her appendix, will continue to be "the best leading actress of the American comedy, thanks to whose intelligence the vulgar and proletarian appendicitis has been elevated to the high status of a presidential ailment" (150). The author metaparodies the Peronist regime and the jirafa "closes" within the norm of *bad acting*. This jirafa demonstrates that the author, even when confronted with the most immediate types of journalistic hypotexts, is capable of hypertextualizing and exposing them to the unavoidable interaction with other hypotexts and discourses.

In "The President's Barber" (March 16, 1950), the author discusses the conservative president of Colombia, Mariano Ospina Pérez, 1946-1950, who had to contend with the Bogotazo and the ensuing violence. The publication date of the jirafa situates it in the period of growing political instability and increasing censorship which severely restricted the printed word. The government of Ospina Pérez undertook a series of large-scale programs to improve economic conditions for the rural sector and to develop national industry, and the photograph which appears in a government newspaper shows the president during "the dedication ceremony of direct telephone service between Bogotá and Medellín" (216). This journalistic hypotext of an official event serves as a point of departure. To hypertextualize the photograph, the author proceeds to dismantle this linear discourse through pictural discourse in which "the context of the author attempts to break up the compactness and closure of the other's discourse, to absorb it, to erase its borders."[46] He accomplishes this by incorporating the heteroglossia of the newspaper readers. The photo conveys an impression of presidential efficiency since the president is surrounded by a battery of phones, and "its seems that each receiver communicated with one of the different problems of state and that the president was forced to spend twelve hours a day trying to direct them by long distance from his remote commander in chief's office" (216).

The author replaces the official discourse of the photograph with his own version of the president being far removed from the public, and then he foregrounds the president in another jirafa-photo: "And in reality, this is the question that I have asked myself while contemplating the last photograph of the best shaved leader in Latin America: Who is the Palace barber?" (216). This hypertextualization of the photo enables the author to introduce a series of observations dealing with the members of the president's official entourage. While "the president's chef must be an official of irrevocable ideological conviction," and his ministers "are men of complete confidence" it is the president's barber who is the most important member because he can "allow himself the democratic freedom of caressing the president's chin with the sharp blade of a barber's razor" (216-17). The fact that the chef and the barber are among the most important member's of the presidential staff illustrates the importance of the system of millimetric politics in Colombia in which every job, from the garbage collector to the president, depends on one's political affiliation. By imprinting a new semantic orientation on the official discourse, the author breaks the closed contours of the photographic reality while retaining the political dimension. The interfacing of politics with the discourse of the reader's imagination allows the author to insert political subjects in a narrative form: "Many times the fate of a republic depends more on a single barber than on all its leaders, as in the majority of cases---according to the poet---that of geniuses depends on the midwife" (217).

The jirafa not only hypertextualizes the official photo but also intertextualizes with it in the same jirafa: "Señor Ospina knows it and perhaps because of that, before leaving to dedicate the direct telephone service between Bogotá and Medellín, the president, with eyes shut and legs stretched out, surrendered to the pleasure of feeling the cold and ironic contact of the razor very near to his jugular vein, while in his mind all the complicated problems that he would have to resolve during the day were passing in quick succession" (217). Once again, confronting the imminency of political hypotexts, which require an immediate and finalized answer in journalistic writing because they succeed one another so rapidly, the author overcomes these limitations to create a jirafa which can interact with other texts.

One of the most significant political jirafa's is "The Waistcoat" (November 28, 1950) in which several fundamental hypotexts converge and clash. This hypotextual conjunction results in a hybrid text in which politics, economics and literature merge to create a microworld that already defines and lays the foundations of the principal setting of many of his future works. This jirafa does not constitute a mere pre-text; rather it is a text written at a specific moment which arises from a bundle of relations present at the time in which he wrote it. The first hypotext is the series of notes that the author wrote for his unfinished novel he was to call *The House*. In these notes the author adumbrates the surrounding contours of the town in which the Buendía house would be situated, but its definitive shape will emerge in successive jirafas. In "The Buendía's House" (June 3, 1950), the author alludes to the town: "Outside there was the town, with its heat and sounds."[47] García Márquez does not fully develop the space of the town in his columns because he is creating his fictional space from the inside out. However, in "The Waistcoat," the spatial parameters of the town expand rapidly: "People led a more carefree existence in that time when cities were starting to emerge and---without completely being towns nor cities---they were composed of two streets running parallel to the river, where there was enough room for three shops, a canteen with an old billiard table and a sawmill. For that reason, it was known that it would be founded as a city and not as a town because it had a sawmill where a boat would dock from time to time" (513). The town/city axis suggests that time and space will combine into a chronotope (the fusion of time and space), a crucial moment in the transformation of the hypotexts that the author has been exploring and transforming into hypertexts in his jirafas. The town/city chronotope presents a bifocal perspective which is both historical and transhistorical.[48] The allusion to "that time" refers to an epoch in which towns existed in relative isolation and developed according to their internal rhythms. Many of these towns continued to thrive completely detached from the spatiotemporal link with the modern world which was extolling the virtues of progress. The city represents the invasion of progress and the vertiginous transformation of the town into an entity which is alien to its inhabitants. The sawmill embodies the idea of progress, a sign of the transition from rural to urban life.

The sawmill forms part of the economic hypotext that was operating in Colombia at that time. This hypotext is constantly present in the work of García Márquez, and it takes the form of the struggle between the internal development of these towns and the external development imposed on them by governments in the name of progress. This dilemma cannot be easily resolved, and the author does not offer an economic blueprint which guarantees the self-determination and integrity of these towns. In a general sense, the economic hypotext of the town/city axis in the jirafa reflects the whole economic history of the continent with its interminable boom and bust cycles of the extractive economy of the 19th and 20th centuries. Under the banner of "order and progress," Latin

American governments allowed the developed countries to come in and extract gold, silver, copper, nitrate, and other natural resources. After the mineral was exhausted, and after the governments had received their cut, the inhabitants of these forlorn towns were left empty-handed, with only the bitter pill of nostalgia to sustain them. The economic development of Colombia and, for that matter, of the whole continent, has been uneven and fragmentary, and it has almost always benefitted the empowered sector of society. In general, the economic policies of these countries, instead of promoting and supporting the equal participation of all segments of society in the creation of the national wealth, redistribute the existing national wealth among those who control the power. To exclude the large majority of the population who live in the towns, governments have created layer upon layer of Kafkaesque bureaucracy to *legally* prevent them from either gaining access to the national wealth or actively producing economic wealth within the legal framework. The economic hypotext is closely associated with the political hypotext, since the same government creates the labyrinthine bureaucracy which excludes the poor from the so-called benefits of progress. In this jirafa, the author is indirectly denouncing the Colombian government of the period which had adopted this policy. The transformation from town to city cannot be effectuated without the support and intervention of the government.

In this town where there is sufficient space for three shops, a canteen and a sawmill, this last element enables progress to invade the town. The sawmill differs from the other components of the town because it can produce economic wealth; that is, the sawmill can generate wealth in different economic systems. The sawmill also has strong ties to the outside world because "from time to time a boat would dock" (513). Finally, it is an economic unit which can function within the framework of a town or a city. Evidently, the sawmill wishes to expand its operations beyond the boundaries of town. The desire to go beyond the limits of the town manifests itself in the class distinctions linked to the town/city axis. The men of the town "were honest workers who did their jobs to make it through the week and on Saturdays they got drunk until they couldn't see straight, certain that only price they would have to pay for their weekend drinking sprees was a well deserved hangover or, in the worst case, a stormy session with their spouses. But nothing more" (513). Neither the town nor the city has a name in this jirafa, and the author is describing a process which is taking place in all the towns which are turning into cities. The components which make up these human entities are also generic. The working class has nothing in common with the rising capitalist bourgeoisie which is starting to form around the economic activity of the sawmill:

> For the son of the sawmill owner and his associate's daughter, there was an open carriage in which vertigo replaced the strategic darkness of modern theaters. The future owners of the sawmill would go out for a ride on Sunday afternoons, he with his finely twirled mustache, a short smock and a fancy vest which was adorned with an oversized watch chain that served the dual purpose of looking at the watch and scaring dogs when the generally convincing argument of the walking stick failed; and she with her starched petticoat and a straw hat pulled down over her ears, under a parasol that did not provide any shade but which at the time was little more than an organ naturally joined to the feminine anatomy" (513).

This couple exemplifies the new economic order that is supplanting that of the town, and the young people lived completely disconnected from the life of the town. The objects which they display (short smock, fancy vest, watch chain, starched petticoat, straw hat and parasol) represent material signs of the profit motive which characterizes this new class. The objects turn into specular bibelots, symbols of the accumulation of wealth. The young couple can parade around the town in their open carriage without the slightest awareness of the town's existence.

This new wealth opens the way for the specular display of their new status: "In the open carriage, to the rhythm of the clip-clop that the affected French dandy left as he passed by, he forgot the countless efforts he made to fasten the full-length breeches to his ankles and she forgot the laborious sacrifice of getting into her invulnerable, iron-ribbed, umbrella-shaped corset, which made her four or five kilos heavier, but also for or five kilos more shapely and attractive" (513-14). The objects lose their human value and only serve to spectacularize the existence of the young couple. These objects distance them from the town's life, and this new economic order produces empty and specular objects. The new owners and heirs of this system transform themselves into passive spectators of the rapid change: "Twice a month they would go to watch the semi-monthly event of the arrival of the boat which brought Japanese parasols and folding screens, Chinese porcelain and American records" (514). The young people immerse themselves in the pullulation of imported objects, but they do not produce anything in this new order. The objectal bedazzlement prevents them from seeing and participating in the town's life: "Intoxicated by the fin-de-siècle romanticism, they did not even notice that in the bar two men who were playing pool, stabbed each other to death and killed two bystanders in the process in a final and dramatic outburst" (514). These young people live in a reality of simulacra and simulation in which objects offer them an infinite series of specular fascinations.

If the town and the city stand diametrically opposed from an economic standpoint, their political systems are also different. The author calls into question the economic policies of the conservative government which in 1950 undertook in earnest the large scale economic development of the country. This meant the rapid and massive infusion of foreign capital in the name of progress. García Márquez does not seem to oppose the idea of progress so much as the blatantly exploitative application of progress which transforms the towns without creating a structure which insures its continuation for the benefit of the inhabitants. As this jirafa shows, the towns are generally stripped of everything, and the benefits accrue to those who already possess the lion's share of the economic wealth. If the author situates his jirafa at the beginning of the twentieth century, it is because this process had already been in operation for a long time, perhaps even dating back to the independence of the continent. These towns occupy a different spatiotemporal zone, and the linear time of progress does not respect this position in its constant drive to transform everything that it finds in its path.

Beyond the transformation of the economic and political hypotexts, the author establishes the town as the principal setting of his fiction. He gives a generic portrait of the town which encompasses all the towns invaded by progress. This irresistible force situates the towns in the twilight zone in which they are cut off from the past and cannot advance into the future. These towns have to satisfy themselves with the bitter pill of nostalgia, with existing in a temporal vacuum in which they continue to deteriorate and fall apart until they reach complete immobility and isolation. This jirafa marks an important step in the handling of the hypotexts, and its content extends far beyond the finalization and immediate answer which journalism requires. This jirafa succeeds in combining and synthesizing a group of hypotexts that, at first glance, appear radically different.

In "Something Resembling a Miracle" (March 15, 1952), the author returns to the costeño culture hypotext when he visits the town of La Paz in the Department of the Magdalena. The transformation of the hypotext is accomplished through transmotivation. The ostensible theme of the jirafa is the violence and the effects of political repression which have silenced the voices and music of the town: "I do not know if it was my good luck---from my perspective as a simple tourist---or an unfortunate situation, from another standpoint, that several days ago when I arrived in La Paz, in the Magdalena, I had found that an atmosphere of martial law still prevailed there, a result of certain bitter episodes which transpired more than a month ago, and to which newspapers all over the country gave wide coverage" (712). The author demotivates this theme immediately, concentrating instead on another aspect of the town: "La Paz---as its name indicates---is a town of humble and quiet people, a farming community where you have to go if you want to listen to vallenata music in its original form and natural setting" (712). The author remotivates the jirafa by replacing the political theme with a fundamental element of costeño culture---music: "In La Paz, everybody sings from birth, in any place and at any time" (712). This substitutive transformation enables the author to confront the political hypotext in an oblique manner and to criticize the censorship that always accompanies political repression. Music forms part of the heteroglossia that the centripetal forces always attempt to silence, and the author adamantly opposes this power in all its forms. Transmotivation affords him the opportunity to subvert the censorship: "The most remarkable thing I have to report is that when I arrived in La Paz it had been exactly one month since the last person had been heard singing. Over the ruins of twenty-four destroyed houses, the men had folded up their accordions, and the women had taken refuge in the melancholic and taciturn silence that follows great catastrophes" (712-13). By adopting the perspective of a tourist, the author can express his surprise in the face of this disaster. The motive of the trip---to listen to vallenata music---allows him to discuss politics because in La Paz he does not find anything but ominous silence, the outcome of violence.

Frequently, García Márquez introduces an outside agent who arrives in the town and starts to transform it. The author serves as the catalyst that will initiate the subversion of the silence: "Finally, a little before eight, the silence made it seem that it was already midnight, we decided to use every means at our disposal to convince the accordionist Pablo López to allow us to listen to him play a little music" (713). At first, the false silence of the political repression prevents him from playing, but slowly the town rediscovers its voice, and it starts to break the speechlessness imposed on it by the official world. Pablo says to one of his friends: "'Good, my boy, bring me the accordion and we'll see what happens'" (713). Once the silence is shattered, the town recovers its vitality and "Pablo López played like never before in his life" (713).

Music undermines the silence, and the voice of Pablo López combines with the collective voice of the town: "And then everybody who came was singing. And the women sang. And at midnight, when we left Pablo López, still bent over his accordion, we suddenly found ourselves in a completely different town. And in another place, in the recently reawakened town, there were two or three men sitting on their doorsteps playing their accordions. The shops were all lit up and in the middle of the square, you could hear the discordant voice of a drunk loudly singing the latest paseo of Rafael Escalona" (713-14). Music, as a subversive element, has triumphed over violence and political repression in this jirafa, and it enables the author to criticize the forces which try to suppress the human heterophony. This jirafa shows that García Márquez does not avoid politics; rather his confrontation with politics follows a more indirect route and he succeeds in undermining these repressive forces by unleashing other heteroglossia which conflict and oppose the monoglottic voice of authority.

These political jirafas reveal García Márquez's subversive approach which consists of finding the weak point of every political monoglossia; that is, the same monolithic and rigid unitary voice of authority which seeks to co-opt all the other voices and speak for them. García Márquez exposes the impossibility of this goal because, sooner or later, this authoritarian voice must combine with other voices which modify and distort it, and, in many cases, subvert it. He also realizes that this is a continuous and constant process, and that a definitive victory is rarely achieved. García Márquez's approach to politics is a subversive act because it liberates the voices silenced by antihuman forces. In each one of the political jirafas, he introduces a subversive element that opposes the repressive power. These components can take various forms, but their diversity reflects the same social diversity that gives rise to a multitude of voices.

Cultural Jirafas With Intertextual and Autotextual Relations

In two cultural jirafas, "A Visit to Santa Marta" and "The Statues of Santa Marta" (March 1 and 2, 1950), García Márquez returns to his favorite hypotext, costeño culture. This time he explores the costeño ambience of the city of Santa Marta, and reveals his antipathy for the colonial cities of the interior. In the case of Santa Marta, which he progressively transforms into a generic place, we must distinguish between the concepts of place and space. The idea of place "is related to the physical, mathematically measurable shape of spatial dimensions. Of course, in fiction, these places do not actually exist, as they do in reality. But our imaginative faculty dictates that they be included in the fabula".[49] As Mieke Bal explains, the story "is determined by the way in which the fabula is presented. During this process, places are linked to certain points of perception. These places seen *in relation to their perceptions* are called space. That point of perception may be a character, which is situated in space, observes it, and reacts to it. There are three senses which are especially involved in the perception of space: *sight, hearing,* and *touch.*"[50] The author transforms the hypotext of Santa Marta-place through transvaluation, a technique which also includes devaluation and revaluation.

The author immediately devalues the city of Santa Marta as a place: "A welcome invitation kept me away for several days from these extremely pleasant surroundings. Fortunately I was in a city---Santa Marta---where each centenary stone, each monument, each moment of the beautiful bay is one more reason to keep this daily windmill of impressions turning" (191). The author clearly signals his intention to provide the reader with his perceptions of Santa Marta not as a physical place, but as a space perceived through various sensory channels. This transformation will create an intertextual relation between place and space that he will carry out in an eidetic form through his windmill of impressions. The first sense which he emphasizes is that of hearing: "The truth is that Santa Marta is a disturbingly silent city. Perhaps the most silent one that I have known with the exception of Tunja, Popayán, Cartagena, Mampós, and all those small towns of the interior of the country where the visitor has sufficient cause to ask himself whether he is really a living person or a ghost" (191). The dichotomy in the work of García Márquez between the coast and the interior clearly emerges in this jirafa: "The landlocked cities of Tunja and Popayán, resemble an uninhabited monastery more than towns" (191). Santa Marta "has an ambience that seems to live in the past century even though its architectural appearance does not preserve the colonial influence of Tunja, Popayán and Cartagena" (191). Santa Marta's architecture does not convert the city into a dusty museum devoid of its human element, and within its confines the past and present can coexist in a chronotopic relationship: "In Santa Marta in each large old house there is a historical marker and a piano lesson. Forever" (192).

The devaluation of the historical content of Santa Marta's architecture opens the way for the revaluation of the city as a human space. This transvaluation coincides with García Márquez's primary fictional space, which is usually a remote place in which architecture does not play a prominent role. The key to the problem is the previous distinction drawn between place and space. A remote, unknown place offers more possibilities to create a space than a well-defined and famous one with which the readers are able to identify easily and whose familiarity could limit their ability to involve themselves in it. The generic places-spaces like Macondo lack a definite architectural style because they might otherwise be too closely associated with a specific historical period.

Alejo Carpentier affirms that "the great difficulty of using our cities as settings for novels lies in the fact that our cities *do not have a style*."[51] What they contain is "a *third style*: the style of things which do not have any style."[52] This third style "is usually ignored by those who see it every day" and, consequently, "very few of our cities have been *revealed up to now*."[53] For Carpentier, revealing a city corresponds to the project carried out by the Surrealists in Paris in works like Louis Aragon's *The Peasant of Paris* (1926) in which the narrator wanders about Paris transforming cafes, monuments and other well-known places into Surrealist spaces. Paris, however, offers a ready-made cityscape replete with architectural wonders to be transformed, whereas Latin American cities lack this architectural unity since they are usually strange mixtures of imported styles. Carpentier describes an urban section of Havana where "all sorts of imaginable styles intermingle: counterfeit Greek, Roman, Renaissance, false chateaux of the Loire Valley, false Rococo, and false *modern style*."[54]

Latin American cities are composed successive layers of imitated, imported and ultimately useless architectural styles which convert them into spaces which are alien to Latin American reality. To *reveal* the city, the novelist must look beyond the architectural hodgepodge and see how chronotopic relationships function in them. Many Latin American cities encompass an array of different time zones within their boundaries, ranging from prehistoric to utopian: "In Latin America everything is outsized and disproportionate: towering mountains and waterfalls, endless plains, impenetrable jungles. An anarchic urban spread overlies breathless virgin expanses. The ancient rubs elbows with the new, the archaic with the futuristic, the technological with the feudal, the prehistoric with the utopic. In our cities skyscrapers stand side by side with Indian markets that sell totemic amulets. How to make sense of this profusion---of a world whose crushing presence dwarfs man, confuses his senses, staggers his understanding and imagination?"[55] The writer's task is to integrate the different architectural styles with the spatialized temporal zones of the city, to arrive at a chronotopic synthesis of these elements.

García Márquez's distinct preference for cities located on Colombia's Atlantic coast also relates to their openness to the sea. Santa Marta's bay "is a feeling. A peaceful feeling of quietude, well-being and gentleness. It could be said---because of its extraordinary beauty---that it is not a landscape, but an optical illusion" (192). Whether it is a cityscape or a seascape, García Márquez seeks to *reveal* them in a manner advocated by Carpentier. Santa Marta's silence and the magnificent stillness of the bay emanate from the inhabitants of the city and the natural setting. This silence is an indigenous element unlike that of Cartagena where "serious measures have been taken by the police in order to eliminate the disorderly noises of the city" (192). The silence which he describes needs no rational explanation and constitutes an integral part of the daily reality in which people live.

This jirafa intertextualizes eidetically with the cultural hypotext of Santa Marta, and the text-space that the author creates, constitutes an autotext which doubles referentially the space of his fiction. The transvaluation of Santa Marta demonstrates that the author, in search of the macroelements of his fiction, discovers most of them in the costeño ambience that represents the most important hypotext of his work. If at this moment García Márquez still has not developed the surrounding environment in which he can situate the Buendía house, the transtemporal aspect of Santa Marta already supplies him with one of the most crucial facets of his fictional space. Santa Marta is already a city and García Márquez prefers towns to those cities whose more advanced stage of development prevents him from using them as settings for his fiction. Moreover, the historical reality of the continent shows that there are many more towns than cities, and García Márquez most likely believed that the town-spaces offered him the best opportunity to recover the totality of human experience and delineate their different stages. We have already seen the start of this process in "The Waistcoat." In any case, Santa Marta seems to have escaped from the prison house of linear time, since the past and the present have combined to form a chronotopic unity.

In "The Statues of Santa Marta," the author intertextualizes with official history to create an intertext of the human history of the city. The author uses transvaluation to carry out the transformation of the hypotext of official history. Like the previous jirafa, he starts to devalue the symbols of historical validity---its statues: "If I had traveled a lot, I would venture to say that the strangest statues in the world are those of Santa Marta" (192). The author begins to defamiliarize reality and the atmosphere surrounding the statues in order to prepare the reader for the transvaluation of the statues. The arrival of the author on a carnival Tuesday coincides with the defamiliarization of reality, and "some last minute partygoers wearing masks were still walking through the streets without any notion of time" (192). This temporal concurrence allows the author to reshuffle the linear and historical time of Don Rodrigo de Bastidas, the founder of Santa

Marta: "Perhaps for that reason I was not surprised to see a monumental caballero facing the bay, decked out in all the trappings of the Spanish conquistador, who seemed to be parading all his annoyance of an ignored person in disguise. In reality, I thought that one must have an unquestionable patriotic spirit to put on all that military gear when it was 85° in the shade and to start walking around aimlessly at the edge of the sea" (193). The historical space of Don Rodrigo aspires to stasis, permanence, solidity, whereas the daily space of the people is filled with movement, instability and constant change. In this daily space, time loses its linear flow. The monoglottic discourse of Don Rodrigo is now sullied by the discourse of popular culture, and one day someone decided to put the statue "on solid ground, with its back to the bay and ten centimeters above sea level" (193). Don Rodrigo has thus cast off his "antiquated and severe statue personality and he is changing into a historical passer-by, one of the old men of the city who goes to seashore every afternoon to watch time and the girls pass by" (193).

This jirafa dichotomizes official and popular culture which constantly encroaches on the space of official history. This intertextualization leads to the copresence of two texts, to the presence of one text in another. This autotext anchored in popular culture resembles the space which the author will continue to develop in his fiction, but it is already present in his jirafa. The transformation and transvaluation of the statue of Don Rodrigo stem from the desire of one Doctor Augusto Ramírez Moreno who "prophesied in a spectacular diatribe, that even Don Rodrigo himself would turn his back to the diaphanous and tranquil seascape" (193). Consequently, "from that moment on the founder stepped down from his pedestal, went walking away in a melancholy mood and turned his back on the scenic landscape, just to please Doctor Ramírez Moreno" (193). The defamiliar becomes the norm in the carnivalesque space of popular culture, and "the founder is certainly more human, more familiar, and his household popularity has increased quite a bit!" (193).

The author continues to intertextualize with these statues by examining another almost mythical figure of Latin American history, Simón Bolívar. Bolívar does not interest García Márquez so much for his historical role as for the curious way in which his "statue appears in a public square with the same measurements of those desk top Bolívars which simultaneously and unfortunately serve as private monuments and paperweights" (193-94). The author demonumentalizes Bolívar and his historical stature. This is an act of bravado in a country where Bolívar is an obsession for historians and "placed in the shadow of a small temple, the statuette of Bolívar has its miniaturized history" (194).

Another strange statue is "a completely Greek statue, also of small dimensions, and full of marmoreal tunics and Hellenic profiles, like a symbol of something that no one has been able to explain" (194). Despite its inexplicable presence, the statue occupies a perfectly logical place within the space of popular culture: "But like all of them, it too has its history in Santa Marta. And it seems that during one carnival the illuminated fountains spouted wine instead of water, which was simultaneously a waste and an exquisite expression of paganism" (194). The author devalues the statues in their historical dimension in order to revalue them in the realm of popular culture. The defamiliar becomes the natural state of things, and the author can reaffirm: "For that reason I believe that the statues of Santa Marta are the strangest ones that I have known" (194).

These two jirafas represent an autotext, a *mise-en-abyme* of the fictional universe whose dimensions the author will constantly expand. It is important to note that the author is carrying out this transformation in a city and not a town, which will be the primary setting of his works. If a writer only writes one work, then the town will represent, from his unfinished novel, *The House*, to *OHYS*, his primary fictional space. These two jirafas bring out the conflict between two concepts of time---historical and mythic---and García Márquez is still vacillating between these two poles. His transformation of the statues already indicates his firm opposition to official history which he will constantly strive to undermine in his work. Therefore, it is not surprising that he chooses to transvalue the statues because the hypotext of the official history of Santa Marta does not contain the new values that he attributes to them in the jirafas. In "The Waistcoat," García Márquez succeeds in creating an authentic generic place-space in which politics, history, economic and, to a lesser degree, mythic time, coalesce into a whole. Santa Marta already has a history and an identity which reduce the possibility of transforming it on a large scale, but the process is starting to function.

The analysis of the jirafas published in *El Heraldo* show the importance of transtextual relations, especially hypertextuality. Unlike much of his fiction of the period, García Márquez draws on the hypotexts related to his personal experience in his journalism; that is, costeño culture, the politics and history of Colombia, and his participation in the Group of Barranquilla. These hypotexts lay the permanent foundations of the continuous transformations that he will carry out, first in his journalism and then in his fiction. Besides representing the cutting edge of the most important transformations, the jirafas surpass the confined space of the column and the limitations of immediacy and finalized answers to interconnect with each other and become assimilated to the infinite Text that the author is writing. Consequently, these jirafas cannot be classified according to a specific type of journalism. Moreover, the interplay of the transtextual relations in these pieces contributes to the author's bigeneric writing. The jirafas also demonstrate the subversive method that the author uses to undermine the political positions and history of the official world. He realizes the futility of creating yet another official version of a political or historical event, but he can subvert them by liberating the many voices and heteroglossia which surround the official accounts. It is in this sense that García Márquez is a realist, because he does not arbitrarily suppress the monoglossia of official culture. Above all, these early journalistic texts invigorate and strengthen the fundamental hypotexts of his costeño heritage and progressively modify, displace and/or integrate the external cultural demons that he adopted in his first short stories.

Notes

1. Gabriel García Márquez, *Obra periodística Vol 1: Textos costeños*, ed. Jacques Gilard (Barcelona: Bruguera, 1981), 20. Translation is mine.

2. Richard Weiner, *Webster's New World Dictionary of Media and Communications* (New York: Simon & Schuster, 1990), 57.

3. Pedro Sorela, *El otro García Márquez: Los años difíciles* (Madrid: Mondadori, 1988), 29. All translations are mine.

4. Gabriel García Márquez, *Textos costeños*, 249. All other quotes from the jirafas come from this work, and page numbers will be given in parentheses in the text. All translations are mine.

5. Sorela, *El otro García Márquez*, 17-18.

6. Germán Vargas, *Sobre literatura colombiana* (Bogotá: Fundación Simón y Lola Guberek, 1985), 127-28. All translations are mine.

7. Germán Vargas, *Sobre literatura colombiana*, 197.

8. Sorela, *El otro García Márquez*, 21-2.

9. Sorela, 23.

10. Antonio López de Zuazo Algar, *Diccionario del periodismo* (Madrid: Ediciones Pirámide, 1985), 201. All translations are mine.

11. Alvaro Pineda Botero, *Teoría de la novela* (Bogotá: Plaza y Janés, 1987), 57. All translations are mine.

12. Alvaro Pineda Botero, 61.

13.   At the end of his latest novel, *The General in His Labyrinth*, García Márquez, in a section entitled "Gratitudes," thanks all those people who helped him to research different facets of the life of Simón Bolívar: "This book would not have been possible without the help of those who explored all these areas before me during the last century and a half, and who facilitated the literary temerity of narrating a life enveloped in an enormous mass of documentation, and without abandoning the boundless laws of the novel. The Colombian historian, Eugenio Gutiérrez Cely, in response to a questionnaire of many pages, compiled an extensive card file which not only furnished me with many surprising facts---many of which were buried and forgotten in the Colombian newspapers of the 19th century---but also gave me the first ideas about a method for researching and organizing my information." Translation is mine. (*El general en su laberinto* Bogotá: La Oveja Negra, 1989, 270). He continues to enumerate his many sources, and he reconfirms his need to research completely his topic before writing. This tendency dates back to his work as an investigative reporter for *El Espectador* in 1954-55.

14.   Gérard Genette, *Palimpsestes: La Littérature au Second Degré* (Paris: Editions du Seuil, 1982), 12. All translations are mine.

15.   Gérard Genette, *Palimpsestes*, 428.

16.   Genette, *Palimpsestes*, 315.

17.   Genette, *Palimpsestes*, 393.

18.   Genette, 257.

19.   Genette, 304.

20.   Genette, 29.

21.   Pedro Sorela, *El otro García Márquez*, 52.

22.   Sorela, 52.

23.   In García Márquez's series "Traveling Through the Socialist Countries: 90 Days Behind the 'Iron Curtain,'" (Bogotá: La Oveja Negra, 1986), 79, he expresses one of his more irreverent views: "In Auschwitz there is an exhibit of those articles and one can understand that this sinister industry had a bright economic future: a suitcase made out of human skin is of high quality. I did not believe that a man's usefulness could also include being used to make suitcases." Translation is mine. Some would immediately say that García Márquez's attitude, in the face of this incomprehensible human barbarity, reveals complete insensitivity. On the contrary, it expresses a profound understanding of the human dimension of the tragedy. The hypotext is so horrible that the only possible answer is humor. Although humor can function as a defense mechanism, it enables the author to confront and surpass the situation in purely human terms. This is another way of stating that García Márquez never avoids reality, but there are many ways of confronting it.

24.   The bricoleur is a "man who undertakes odd jobs and is a Jack of all trades or a kind of professional do-it-yourself man." Claude Lévi-Strauss, *The Savage Mind* (Chicago: Univ. of Chicago Press, 1970), 17.

25.   Gérard Genette, *Palimpsestes*, 451.

26.   Genette, 453.

27.   *Webster's II New Riverside University Dictionary* (Boston: Houghton Mifflin Company, 1984), 1174.

28.   The train resurfaces in *OHYS* and is described in an identical manner: "'It's coming,' she finally explained. 'Something frightful, like a kitchen dragging a village behind it.'" Gabriel García Márquez, *One Hundred Years of Solitude*, trans. Gregory Rebassa (New York: Avon, 1972), 210.

29.   See footnote 2, Chapter 2, page 31.

30. Gabriel García Márquez, *The Fragrance of Guava*, trans. Ann Wright (London: Verso, 1983), 30.

31. In García Márquez's acceptance speech in Stockholm, Sweden in 1982, he refers to Faulkner in the same manner: "On a day like today, my master William Faulkner said: 'I refuse to accept the end of man.'" Gabriel García Márquez, *La soledad de América Latina* (Cali: Corporación Editorial Universitaria de Colombia, 1982), 12. Translation is mine.

32. Mikhail Bakhtin, *Problems of Dostoevsky's Poetics*, trans. Caryl Emerson (Minneapolis: Univ. of Minnesota Press, 1984), 127.

33. Aden Hayes, "Hemingway y García Márquez: Tarde o temprano," 53, published in: *Violencia y literatura en Colombia*, ed. Jonathan Tittler (Madrid: Editorial Orígenes, 1989). Translations are mine.

34. See pages 53-57 of the article by Aden Hayes for a detailed discussion of the different points of contact between the two writers.

35. Aden Hayes, "Hemingway y García Márquez," 57.

36. Pedro Sorela, *El otro García Márquez*, 53.

37. See footnote 25, page 70.

38. Pedro Sorela, *El otro García Márquez*, 47.

39. Pedro Sorela, 48.

40. M. M. Bakhtin, *The Dialogic Imagination: Four Essays*, trans. Caryl Emerson and Michael Holquist (Austin: Univ. of Texas Press, 1981), 429.

41. Pedro Sorela, 50.

42. Wolfgang Iser, *The Act of Reading: A Theory of Aesthetic Response* (Baltimore: The Johns Hopkins UP, 1978), 101.

43.　Gerald Prince, *Dictionary of Narratology* (Lincoln: University of Nebraska Press, 1989), 85.

44.　Gerald Prince, 85.

45.　Gerald Prince, 85.

46.　Tzvetan Todorov, *Mikhail Bakhtin: The Dialogical Principle*, trans. Wlad Godzich (Minneapolis: The Univ. of Minnesota Press, 1984), 69.

47.　Gabriel García Márquez, *Obra periodística Vol. 1: Textos costeños*, 891.

48.　Michael Holquist discusses this idea in his book, *Dialogism: Bakhtin and his World* (London: Routledge, 1990), 109-115. He adds that the "chronotope, like most terms characteristic of dialogism, must be treated 'bifocally,' as it were: invoking it in any particular case, one must be careful to discriminate between its use as a lens for close-up work and its ability to serve as an optic for seeing at a distance" (113).

49.　Mieke Bal, *Narratology: Introduction to the Theory of Narrative*, trans. Christine van Boheemen (Toronto: Univ. of Toronto Press, 1985), 93.

50.　Mieke Bal, *Narratology*, 93-4.

51.　Alejo Carpentier, *Tientos y diferencias* (Buenos Aires: Calicanto Editores, 1976), 14. Translations are mine.

52.　Alejo Carpentier, 16.

53.　Alejo Carpentier, 17.

54.　Alejo Carpentier, 15.

55. Luis Harss and Barbara Dohmann, *Into the Mainstream: Conversations With Latin American Writers* (New York: Harper & Row, 1967), 39-40.

Chapter 4

Journalistic Peregrinations III:
The Bogota Phase, 1954-1955

Introduction: Cachaco Land, **El Espectador** *and New Directions*

García Márquez's journalistic peregrinations turn inland from
the luminous land of the Caribbean towards Bogotá, the domain of
the cachacos, a name that the costeños apply to the inhabitants of
these landlocked, somber cities. From February, 1954 to July,
1955, García Márquez worked in Bogotá as a member of the staff
of the Liberal newspaper, *El Espectador*. There exists a lacuna in
the journalistic biography of the author concerning his joining *El
Espectador*. Jacques Gilard bases his version on the personal
memories of García Márquez:

> García Márquez recalls that, after his brief stint with *El
> Nacional* in Barranquilla, he was invited to spend
> several days in Bogotá by Alvaro Mutis, who was in
> charge of the advertising department for Esso. He
> spent his time in Mutis's office, and at the end of
> several days, he still did not know what he wanted to
> do. At that time, the offices of *El Espectador* were
> located in the same building on the Avenida Jiménez,
> and more than once during that stay that was
> supposed to be very brief, the owners of the
> newspaper asked García Márquez to write short pieces
> "because they needed an editor" to get them out of a
> tight spot. While he was getting bored in Bogotá,
> thinking that he was not doing anything and that he
> was wasting Mutis's time, and he was deciding to
> return to the Coast, the owners of *El Espectador*
> offered him a position as editor with a salary of 900
> pesos a month. The offer and the salary were just too
> enticing, if we consider that he was only paid three
> pesos for each "jirafa" he wrote for *El Heraldo*. With
> 900 pesos not only could he live very comfortably, but

he could also help his parents. The result was that he accepted that job and stayed in Bogotá, when earlier he had not intended to stay away from the Atlantic Coast for very long. Later on he came to suspect that the invitation by Mutis was part of a plot by *El Espectador* to bring him to Bogotá and hire him.[1]

The second version is based on the fact that *El Espectador* had published the first short stories of García Márquez in its Sunday supplement, "Weekender," directed by the then assistant director of the newspaper, Eduardo Zalamea Borda "Ulises":

Ulises stated on one occasion in the supplement, which was highly literary, that there were not any young writers who deserved serious attention in Colombia. And according to Guillermo Cano, the head of *El Espectador*, that is the starting point of García Márquez's association with the newspaper for which he was to work. The young costeño writer took up the challenge made by "Ulises" and sent the story "The Third Resignation" to the supplement. Eduardo Zalamea Borda considered the story of very high quality---as Guillermo Cano says---and he published it in the next issue of the weekend supplement accompanied by a laudatory note about the author. If my memory serves me well, he said that he would be interested in personally meeting the author. Some time later, García Márquez visited Zalamea Borda with several of his friends, some of them known by Zalamea and by us, and regular participants in the literary circle of García Márquez. I would say that at that time we did not know García Márquez's work as a journalist in Cartagena and Barranquilla, but I could not say for sure if his joining the newspaper was the result of a plot hatched by Alvaro Mutis in collusion with someone at the newspaper so that he would get involved with *El Espectador* and then later be asked him to stay on. What is certain is that his link to the paper was the short story and that he was asked to continue with *El Espectador* the same day that we met him as a result of this real episode.[2]

Another account comes from another costeño journalist, Gonzalo González "Gog," a distant relative of García Márquez, linked to magazine *Crónica*, "who at that time was in charge of the section, 'Questions and Answers,' in which he would clear up all sorts of problems for readers. According to 'Gog,' the two previous versions are more literary, and in reality García Márquez's joining *El Espectador* was less complicated. Very simply, someone suggested to him that if they had published his story in the paper, he had a good chance of being hired as an editor. García Márquez tried his luck out and he was hired."[3] These three versions confirm that the author's literary and journalistic biographies intertwine in the same way as his bigeneric writing, and it is difficult to detail the reasons that determine his journalistic debut in *El Espectador*.

The distinguishing features of this brief but significant stage in his career are the new journalistic environment and the diversity of activities to which he would dedicate his time and energy. *El Espectador* "was the second largest newspaper in the country in terms of circulation, after *El Tiempo*, and although like that newspaper it prided itself on its liberal affiliation---that is, one of the two largest traditional political parties in the country---it is perhaps the Colombian newspaper which has continued to keep alive the original premises of its ideology and maintain its independent status."[4] According to Guillermo Cano, the head of *El Espectador*, who was assassinated in 1986 by the drug kingpins' hired killers, the newspaper "was then, as now, a newspaper of liberal ideas, a supporter of the democratic system of individual rights, free elections and social and economic justice."[5] *El Espectador* closely monitored the style of its news, and if García Márquez had already received the literary seal of approval from the assistant director, Zalamea Borda, he still had to satisfy the rigorous standards of the chief editor, José Salgar. Salgar "had and still has the reputation of knowing a good journalist when he sees one, and all the evidence indicates that he saw the journalist in García Márquez, although without exaggerating: According to what he told me in July, 1983, many journalists like the García Márquez of those days---that is, competent young men who performed their work diligently, have worked for *El Espectador*, which in turn prides itself on being a training school for journalists."[6]

According to Sorela, *El Espectador* differed from the costeño newspapers because "its editors were already aware of the adverse effects that language could suffer from the demands of the time pressures of journalism, among other factors, and they tried to maintain a constant vigil in stylistic matters. For example, during that time when linotype was being used, before the introduction of the present computerized printing techniques, the newspaper employed a language specialist as a proof reader. José Salgar remembers that the new journalist, who was soon to become the 'star' editor, was extremely meticulous in matters of style. Always respectful of his bosses, he would carry on a private and furious battle against the commonplace, and would present his original copy in a very neat form."[7]   The journalistic environment of *El Espectador* established more formal parameters than those of the costeño newspapers, and the standards of the newspaper contributed to his development as a writer, especially with respect to his feature stories.

García Márquez's move from the coast to Bogotá also produces a spatial change in his journalism. The longer articles, published in several parts, afforded him the opportunity to develop his writing and narrative techniques in a more coherent way. These longer articles are especially important because the unity of vision of the jirafas still lacked a narrative framework which could enable García Márquez to communicate his totalizing vision in a sustained manner. As Pedro Sorela explains: "In his newspaper reporting García Márquez found exactly what he needed, since what is a newspaper article but a narration, and even more, a narration based on a story. That is exactly what the Colombian writer's narrative style is. Like many other writers before him---such as Hemingway, one of his masters---García Márquez discovered in newspaper articles not only an increased contact with the 'street,'---and in many cases his articles were based on documentation and interviews---but also an area for narrative experimentation, honed by the requirements of mass communications, which would also serve him well in his stories and novels."[8] In this period, then, García Márquez focuses on developing a narrative vehicle through which he can channel his vision. Narration is the key to expanding his vision already present in the jirafas, and he achieves this goal by moving beyond the column format into investigative reporting. As Stephen Minta points out, "García Márquez has often spoken of the stylistic lessons he learned from journalism, more particularly from the time when he began to work as an investigative reporter in 1954. He believes that what he learned, essentially, were the literary equivalents of the oral techniques of story-telling which people like his grandmother possessed in such high degree."[9] The stylistic lessons to which Minta refers constitute solid achievements which will influence his later fiction. These longer journalistic pieces link the vision contained in the jirafas to his later fiction in which the full impact of this early journalism will manifest itself.

García Márquez does not neglect his literary output during this period. In 1954, he won first prize in the National Short Story Contest for "One Day After Saturday" and the following note published in "From Day to Day" section of *El Espectador* confirms the double focus of the young writer's career: "García Márquez (27 years old from Barranquilla) thus continues his admirable career as a writer and journalist, the evidence of which can be seen in the works that we have mentioned as well as in his excellent articles in the "From Day to Day" section of *El Espectador*, and in his perceptive film reviews."[10]

García Márquez's journalistic work for *El Espectador* branches out in three directions: 1) film criticism; 2) short articles written for the "Day to Day" column which present problems of authorship because many were not signed; and 3) feature articles, usually appearing in installments, on topics ranging from a long series on a noted Colombian cyclist to the return of the Colombian soldiers from Korea and their subsequent neglect by the government. García Márquez's film criticism, which appeared regularly except when he was doing investigative reporting, offers less interest for several reasons. For García Márquez, film criticism represented a completely new field in which he lacked training and experience. His critical posture is unquestionably nationalistic and his commentaries often represent an apology for the absence of a thriving Colombian film industry. As Jacques Gilard explains, García Márquez's writing in this area "is a very impressionistic criticism, sometimes based on recent and poorly assimilated knowledge, and not exempt from a naive pedantry. Although the sources that he used would have to be researched more carefully, the influence of his readings of the works of Sadoul is apparent (a French film critic who wrote *The General History of Film*)."[11]

García Márquez's film criticism thus offers a mixture of enthusiasm (as demonstrated by the column's regular appearance during this period under the headings of "Films in Bogotá," "First-Run Films of the Week" or "New Films"), an uneven and most likely rapidly acquired critical focus, a decidedly pro-Colombian anti-Hollywood stance, and some very questionable predilections and distastes for certain films. The third characteristic, his generally antipathetic attitude towards Hollywood and European films (with some notable exceptions) also points to a more fundamental attitude present in his writing from the beginning: the refusal to assume automatically that either Europe, the United States or the Soviet Union occupies any privileged position or enjoys a monopoly on culture, literature, politics, or any other realm of human endeavor. In fact, García Márquez has often criticized the Soviet Union and its brand of socialism, and his independent stance crystallizes in his series entitled "Traveling in the Socialist Countries: 90 Days Behind the Iron Curtain."

García Márquez is clearly developing an independent posture similar to Oswald Spengler's attitude toward civilization in his work, *The Decline of the West*, which has been an important work for Latin American intellectuals.[12] Spengler rejects the idea that certain civilizations are somehow privileged or superior; rather they all follow the same pattern of any living organism: "Every Culture passes through the age-phases of the individual man. Each has its childhood, youth, manhood and old age."[13] For Spengler every culture is situated at some point along this continuum without regard to notions of superiority or inferiority, and none can escape this process. As González Echevarría points outs, "Spengler offers a view of universal history in which there is no fixed center, and where Europe is simply one more culture. From this arises a relativism in morals and values: no more acculturation of blacks, no need to absorb European civilization. Spengler provided the philosophical ground on which to stake the autonomy of Latin American culture and deny its filial relation to Europe. Spengler's cyclic conception of the history of cultures kindled the hope that if Europe was in decline, Latin America must be then in an earlier, more promising stage of her own independent evolution."[14] While there is no evidence that García Márquez either read Spengler or openly embraced his philosophical tenets, his evolving position vis-a-vis Europe, the United States and the Soviet Union certainly coincides with Spengler in that Latin America in general, and Colombia and especially costeño culture in particular, are just as valid and vital as any other culture.

Of the three areas in which García Márquez worked for *El Espectador*, investigative reporting is the most crucial to his writing: "On August 2, 1954, with his story on the landslide which took place in Medellín, García Márquez initiates a phase of higher output. When he already has a little more than six years of work as a journalist behind him, he becomes a reporter. In many subsequent interviews he emphasized the decisive influence that his work as a reporter had on him."[15] While investigative reporting enabled García Márquez to develop a continuous space for his writing, this same space still imposes strict limits in which he must write.

These longer articles resemble the hybrid genre variously labelled "the literature of fact" or "literary nonfiction writing," and which is often identified with the style of writing christened New Journalism. Ronald Weber defines this often confusing genre as a "complex counterpointing of its two constituent elements, history and literature. In actual practice, in the sixties and the seventies that combination has resulted in fact writing based on reporting that frequently employs techniques drawn from the art of fiction to create something of fiction's atmosphere or feeling and that, most important, moves toward the intentions of fiction while remaining fully factual."[16] Another way of defining the subject is, according to Weber, "Donald Pizer's distinction between two kinds of documentary narratives---one exploring a factual event simply as an event (documentary narrative), the other exploring it as meaning (documentary narrative as art)."[17] In the former, the writer accumulates a large amount of factual detail but does not draw any significance from it. In the latter, the writer, "through selection, arrangement, emphasis, and other literary devices, discovers some meaning or theme in his factual material."[18]

García Márquez's investigative reporting combines both factual reporting and literary techniques, and he focuses primarily on the human context in which the events took place, and not on the events themselves. As Weber states, the writer of literary nonfiction "can take us deeply inside people and events," but his ability to do this is more limited than the fiction writer's because "he is finally restrained by his commitment to the facts."[19] García Márquez's articles represent hybridized creations which alternate between journalistic literature and literaturized journalism. What García Márquez chooses to do in these articles is "to stay within the confines of the evidence as it can be known and within those confines to do many of the things fiction writers do."[20] García Márquez also seeks meaning within the limits of the facts. These spatial and factual limitations provide him with a well-delineated framework in which he can develop his writing techniques, themes and a vision of reality which simultaneously respects the facts and transcends them.

This framework is also important because García Márquez not only limits himself to what can be factually demonstrated, but he also does not invent "facts" to fit his purposes. He does not, however, confine himself to a transcription of naked facts. His articles show that he moves interpretatively, not imaginatively, beyond the facts in order to find patterns of human meaning embedded in the events. Human involvement in events fills in and completes the factual, skeletal framework, and this constitutes the overall pattern in most of these articles. In other words, as Weber explains concerning the literary qualities of nonfiction, the writer tries to "find in factual experience some 'tissue of significances,' some 'resonant meanings.'"[21] Accordingly, in García Márquez's articles, journalism and literature combine to produce a synergetic, hybridized form which converts factual events into human events. This chapter concentrates on three longer series which García Márquez wrote as an investigative reporter. Two other series will be treated in chapters 5 and 6.

Extending His Reach: García Márquez's Investigative Reporting

García Márquez explores the human dimensions of a tragic event in "Evaluation and Reconstruction of the Catastrophe in Antioquia," which appeared in three parts on August 2, 3, and 4, 1954. This first venture in investigative reporting establishes a pattern that the author will follow in much of his subsequent journalism and fiction: He investigates an event which has already occurred and has been "interpreted" by the press and official sources. Frequently, he has to confront the official version, which he inevitably opposes and subverts in his own articles. Pedro Sorela explains the circumstances in which García Márquez undertook this first assignment:

> On July 31, 1954, *El Espectador* "announced on page one" the series by its special correspondent García Márquez on the "Evaluation and Reconstruction of the Catastrophe in Antioquia." It was what is known in the Spanish journalese as a "refrito" (literally refried, or in English journalese, a rerun, repeat, rehash or follow-up): a more or less newsworthy story in the Colombian press, an avalanche with victims, a story which the newspapers had widely covered during the previous days. The paper sent García Márquez on his first

assignment to undertake the thankless task of reporting on something that, in principle, had already been fully covered.   Upon arriving in Medellín, the journalist---as he asserts---was just about ready to return and forget his assignment.   His story would have been different.   He did not do it and quite the contrary he returned with his article whose principal characteristics are already announced in the title---*evaluation and reconstruction*---and which would capture the attention of the newspaper's editors when the time came for future assignments.[22]

The terms *evaluation* and *reconstruction* clearly describe the task of the writer, and García Márquez seems to prefer those situations in which the official version has already "impartially" and "objectively" treated the *what* and *how* of an event.   The fundamentally subversive act of Garciamarquian writing always seeks to undermine the official version in the *how* an event occurred, never in the *what*, because he does not wish to create yet another version of the already narrated. From the beginning, he seems to have realized that the weak point of every official account lies in the *how something happened*.   This also explains why political protest in García Márquez always assumes a narrative form.

By concentrating on the *how something occurred*, García Márquez can investigate reality with more freedom than a reporter who is investigating an ongoing event. This preference may seem paradoxical, but many times the pressure of time forces the reporter to limit himself to the *what* without having the opportunity of penetrating the surface reality of the event. The "refrito" offers García Márquez more latitude, considering that an official version already exists which he can subject to the centrifugal forces of heterophony, or the diversity of voices, which was present at the moment of the disaster.   Therefore, he does not have to seek finality, the definitive answer that the reporter normally must reach in his articles. The narrated already possesses a certain finality that García Márquez can expose to the other voices that the official account had excluded. In his reconstruction of the event he does not look for closure but openness, the unfinalization of reality.

This first assignment not only played a key role in the development of the García Márquez's approach to reality, but it also allowed him to perfect his writing techniques: "We can distinguish the ability to synthesize which enables him to express in a condensed form the major aspects of the problem that he was investigating. We can also include the constant sense of humor which allows him to bring out effectively the most complicated elements of a situation. The method of García Márquez the journalist could be summarized by an axiom: Reality is always surprising; first, you have to know how to look, and then how to express it."[23] The space of the news stories expands rapidly, especially in the "refritos," because the young reporter does not have to limit himself to the narrated, which would fit in a still more restricted space. The spatial expansion occurs above all in the narrating where he can develop a variety of narrative possibilities embedded in the voices which have been temporarily silenced by the official version.

The first part, entitled "The Tragedy Started Seventy Years Ago," offers the following condensation of the disaster: "And the danger continues. Carelessness, solidarity and curiosity supplied about fifty victims. 'They didn't heed the warning they were given,' says Father Giraldo. Alirio and Licirio Caro, the surviving children."[24] García Márquez concentrates on a moment just before the disaster which dramatizes the unawareness of the impending doom, a moment in the daily existence of a family whose life will soon be violently disrupted. The family's daily routine is reinforced by the use of the imperfect: "It was a job that they would do three times a week;" "They were living with their mother and four more brothers..." and the father, Guillermo Caro Gallego, "was removing sand to sell from the land of Luis Enrique Burgos, whom he would pay 10 pesos a week for the right to work it" (245). The iterative, durational aspects of the verbs in the imperfect contrast with the one change in the daily routine, when the father "left earlier than usual" (245). The author carefully sprinkles his opening with small details which emphasize the human context: "a house located next to the 'El Espadero' stream; 'La Iguaná,' a stream on the other side of the city (about 10 kilometers)"; and the children headed for the shop called the "'Half Moon', which is the name used for the whole area" (245). This family scene is suddenly and violently disrupted by a series of preterit moments: "He heard a sound, 'like a herd of horses,' and he saw a small avalanche coming down the side of the mountain towards his parents' house. 'We ran to warn people,' says Jorge Alirio, the oldest and most talkative of the children, 'but then we saw that another eruption was coming, bigger than the first one, and rocks and sticks were falling on us in the road.' The children threw themselves to the ground, the avalanche stopped. A minute later we didn't find a single trace of the house" (246).

The use of the imperfect to establish the routine of one family and the preterit to show the sudden, unsuspected effect of the avalanche, enable the author to give the reader a "complete" picture of the disaster with a minimum of words. Alexis Márquez Rodríguez calls this technique "fade-in" or "elliptical merging" in which the journalist presents an event or series of events in such a way that the reader will supply, intuit and complete each scene even though many details have been omitted.[25] Too many details can bore readers whereas too few can render stories uninteresting. To achieve a balance, the journalist needs a language which enhances the reader's capacity to mentally supply deleted information. The author is not interested in the proairetic code to establish the linear sequence of the events which had already been fully treated in other articles. García Márquez activates the hermeneutic code by contrasting the two situations. Roland Barthes divides the hermeneutic code into ten constituent parts or "kernels": theme, formulation, proposal, promise of an answer, snare, ambiguity, suspended answer, partial answer, jammed answer and disclosure.[26] In the first kernel, theme, emphasis is placed on the object which will be the theme of the enigma. The Gestalt image enables García Márquez to underscore the fact that the family and, by extension, the other victims, will become the object-theme of the enigma. The enigma is the cause of the disaster. The family represents the nucleus on which the enigma of the disaster centers and which the author is investigating. The first indicator in the article is the change in routine: "That day, however, Jorge Alirio and Licirio did not eat breakfast with their father, since he left earlier than usual for 'La Iguaná'" (245). This sentence prepares the reader for the disaster without leaving the framework of the family's daily routine.

By concentrating on the members of one family who will fall victim to the disaster, the author uses a technique which Márquez Rodríguez calls the "law of closure," a term from Gestalt psychology in which "a person, in certain situations, tends to perceive entire objects even when they are not whole. That is, mentally we fill in what is missing; or rather, we complete or 'close' the figure."[27] In narrative terms, this means that the writer, and especially the journalist who works in a still more confined space, must use elliptical language and still make the reader feel that he is reading the whole story despite the selective omissions. The opening picture of the Caro family provides a paradigmatic image of the human dimensions of the tragedy which touches many families who cannot be included in the article. In the section entitled "First Results: 5," the listing of the members of the Caro family humanizes and personalizes the event while suggesting the broader scope of the disaster: "Buried by the avalanche were: Marta de Caro, the mother, who 'was going to do laundry' when her two older children saw her for the last time; Ampara, 9, who was sweeping; Solange, 5; Cielo 2, who had just gotten up, and Argemiro, 8 months old, who still had not woke up" (246). This enumeration corresponds to the second kernel of the hermeneutic code, the formulation of the enigma, without any details being given to classify it. The description of what the family members were doing when the disaster struck enables the reader to form a mental picture of a whole group of people caught unaware in the same situation. This impression is further reinforced by a farmer named Rincón, whom the two children ask for help: "Rincón, oblivious to the magnitude of the disaster, answered them in the following way according to the children: 'I am busy now and I don't have a moment to spare'" (246).

The dimensions of the tragedy widen as the news reaches other parts of the city: "When a telephone message was received at 9:00 a.m. in the fire station from the government's office requesting personnel to be sent for the rescue effort, the news was spreading throughout the city" (246). The author maintains his central focus on the human context, and the residents "of the picturesque and winding district of Las Estancias, which looks like a Nativity scene with its houses huddled against the mountain, were all rushing to the site of the catastrophe, jumping fences to shorten the distance" (246). The focus then shifts to a more technical yet contrapuntal statement concerning the knowledge of the disaster: "The engineers and geologists are certain that 50 or 60 years ago, before the road to Rionegro was built, the first large scale landslide must have taken place there. The tragedy started to happen nearly 60 years ago" (246-47). The technical details constitute a kind of proposal, or the third kernel of the hermeneutic code, but these data, which promise an answer (fourth kernel), only deepen the enigma and stress the lack of concern for the tragic consequences on the part of the authorities. This official statement contrasts sharply with the ignorance in which the area's residents were kept. The author tries to create a poignant, human picture of the disaster before revealing this technical explanation, which now takes on an entirely different meaning for readers. This technical insertion also breaks the mounting tension and crystallizes the tragedy in the reader's mind. Attention then focuses on the rescue efforts, and the reader is already prepared for what will follow---another larger, more violent avalanche with dire consequences. The author reiterates the technical explanation by referring to the possibility of still more landslides: "If a new landslide had taken place at that moment, falling on a tightly bunched and unsuspecting crowd of employees, students, workers, farmers, merchants and curiosity seekers, the number of victims would have exceeded a thousand" (247).

To "complete" the picture of the disaster, the author returns to Guillermo Caro Gallego, whom he introduces to the reader on a personal level: "He supported his wife and six children on 120 pesos a month, and he had managed to build a house on rented land that he hoped to buy later on" (248). García Márquez's human context includes a wealth of details which play an important role in our daily existence. When Caro returns to his work site to ask for more volunteers, "they all agreed except one who said 'because Saturday I had taken a laxative'" (248). This minor detail reveals the presence of the many small, but important, forces, habits and customs which shape and structure our daily lives.

The author finishes the portion devoted to Caro by noting that eighteen of the volunteers would never return, and he thus prepares the reader for another chapter in the unfolding tragedy. Despite the real threat of another landslide, the rescue workers persist in trying to locate the missing and dead. This drama contrasts with official callousness in the face of the tragedy: "The only warning that the inhabitants of Medellín received came from Father Giraldo. No official action was taken" (249). Tragedy strikes again, and the description of the weight of the landslide seems to point an accusing finger at the government: "600,000 cubic meters of earth descended violently on the crowd, which was like having the equivalent weight of two national capitols come rushing down the mountain" (250).

In the second installment entitled "Medellín, Victim of Its Own Solidarity," the author again condenses the article into a series of statements: "The city prepared itself to help 10,000 injured people. 'There were 300 chiefs of operations' in the rescue effort. The estimates of the casualty figures. What might have occurred two hours later. The missing and the rescued" (252). The author creates a panoramic view of this "confusing outburst of public spirit, an incredible manifestation of social solidarity" (252). He moves from place to place, like a camera panning over a scene filled with confusing movement: "No less than a thousand people were giving and disobeying orders, shouting through loudspeakers, without any definite sense of purpose" (254). The author then presents a succession of scenes in which people are caught in the grip of forces which exceed their physical and mental capacities to cope. He also quotes an official source which only widens the gap between the two realities: "At present there is a block of nearly

5,000 cubic meters, and because of the cracks and fissures that it shows, from one minute to the next it can move, and with its speed and impact it can cause more movements in the lower parts covered with displaced material" (255). In the technical explanations the author combines two hermeneutic kernels (the snare and ambiguity) which correspond to a statement which can be interpreted in two different ways. Apparently the authorities had already recognized the danger of a landslide a long time ago, but they mis(dis)informed the inhabitants by not telling them anything after the disaster struck. He places this official statement between the scenes of human confusion and the ensuing wakes for the victims.

The detailed account of the aftermath caused by the tragedy is designed to fill in the Gestalt picture the author initially offered to his readers. García Márquez always seeks out the human context which frequently involves life and death. He never attempts to sensationalize the event or shock his readers, and the enumeration of victims portrays the magnitude of the tragedy in human terms: "Six of the total number of victims were students in the 'Beato Salomón' and 'Miguel de Aguinaga' schools for boys and three were from the 'Manuel José Caycedo' school for girls. It's very likely that the majority of them had heard the warnings of Father Octavio Giraldo, when they were heading towards the site of the disaster" (256). Among the victims is "Guillermo Caro who hours before the landslide of 6:15 had his surviving children taken to the house of some relatives in 'El Coco,' where they now live" (256).

The author introduces highly detailed, factual information into his Gestalt picture in order to concretize it for the reader. The mention of Guillermo Caro crystallizes the tragedy in the reader's mind by providing a meticulous microhistory of a typical family which has been affected by the tragedy. The author returns to the beginning of his article by focusing on the Caro family: "Including the family of Guillermo Caro, whose five members were buried by the first landslide and could not be rescued, the total number of known victims reaches 74" (256). The reader is left with a feeling of false security and official neglect: "The site of the tragedy is quiet, life has started up again, and it takes on the deceptive and peaceful appearance that a new landslide won't take place "(256-57). This sentence acts as a proleptic hinting of a future tragedy, an almost fatalistic statement that people will return even though they may again face the danger of losing their lives. In this closure the author posits another beginning, which "involves presenting some events which have already taken place as new ones, as if they were to happen afterwards."[28]

In the last part, the author again combines "evaluation and reconstruction" in an effort to provide exhaustive information while maintaining the human context. The first subheading, "Did an old gold mine cause the tragedy?", focuses the reader's attention on a possible cause, and this is followed by a series of condensed phrases: "Theories of the explosion. How to avoid a new disaster. A family of fifteen left homeless. The man who came to look for death. God, who brings the disease, also provides the cure. Victims" (258). Even though the article does not follow this order, the subheadings capture and hold the reader's attention, especially the last word "victims."

The author supplies readers with just enough information to enable them to form an idea of the extent of the tragedy in technical terms. In this part the author simultaneously offers a *suspended answer* and a *partial answer* (the gold mine), but the technical information only serves to complexify the enigma and bring into question the competence of the authorities. The landslide in Medellín was "not as serious as the one which took place in Envigado twenty years ago and buried a textile factory" (258). These types of geological phenomena are quite common in the region and "larger in scale than those in La Media Luna " (258). Indeed, compared to other areas where similar mud slides have taken place, "the site of La Media Luna did not present an immediate danger" (259). These comparisons, which deemphasize the geological importance of the Media Luna landslide, bring the tragic human consequences into sharper focus.

Among the possible causes of the tragedy, the theory of a former gold mine tunnel receives the most attention: "There is one very widespread version in Medellín: on the top of the hill where the landslides occurred, someone was trying to work a secret gold mine a long time ago" (259). The author immediately supports this theory with expert testimony: "One of the engineers officially appointed to study the terrain, Doctor Contrado Guendica, considers that version quite accurate" (259). This discussion does not produce any concrete explanation, so the reader must confront a series of unanswered questions. The theory of the gold mine corresponds to the ninth element of the hermeneutic code, the *jammed answer*, in which the official explanations fail to provide a definitive solution to the problem. The most immediate and effective response is to "remove the obstruction artificially, drain the area and plant trees" (260), but as the article shows, the official world of studies, recommendations, analyses, and theories differs radically from the human world of the people who must confront these tragedies.

This dichotomy surfaces in the long sentence which begins the section "The Worst Victim": "Precautions which are taken in that regard would certainly help to reduce the possibility of new tragedies, similar to those of La Media Luna, since for such absurd and avoidable reasons situations are repeated like that of Emilia Pérez, widow of Agudelo, who now lives in poverty in Robledo, with 15 more people, because her son, Jesús Gilberto Agudelo, sand dealer, 45, walked 10 kilometers on the afternoon of July 12 to help in the rescue of the Caro family" (260). The hermeneutic code moves toward disclosure (the last kernel), the discovery and enunciation of the meaning, but, evidently, the author does not offer any final answer. The technical information does not help pinpoint the cause of the disaster, and, on the contrary, it complicates the situation. The authorities are concerned above all with finding an official explanation which will relieve them of the necessity of accepting the responsibility for the catastrophe. The technical information suggests that the authorities are guilty of covering up the dangerous situation for a long time. If the authorities can point to a geological or natural cause, they can thus say that there was nothing they could have done to prevent it.

García Márquez strongly distrusts the official world, and he ironically portrays its inability to explain the disaster or take any concrete measures to protect the public. This series demonstrates his method of indirectly subverting the official version of the events. The journalistic "refritos" furnish the author with an open invitation to displace the proairetic code of the events. Unlike the orthodox practice of investigative reporting which seeks to close the hermeneutic code, García Márquez prefers to open up the news event to the channels of dialogic interaction, to the multitude of voices, so that there is no definitive disclosure and he can question the authority and veracity of the official version. By contrast, the daily life of the people resembles the carnivalesque space in which tragedy and comedy coexist with many other paired opposites such as life and death. Jesús Gilberto Agudelo, who belonged to the "Mutual Aid Society of the Virgin of Carmen," came to find life but instead encounters death. One of Emilia Pérez's sons, Julio, wanted to become a sand dealer like his father, but he discovered that he was allergic to sand. These examples reveal the lengths to which García Márquez goes in order to portray the carnivalesque world of daily human existence, and the extreme importance that he attaches to the human context.

Back on Home Ground: Revealing the Chocó

During his investigative reporting for *El Espectador,* García Márquez also expands his knowledge of those components of Colombian reality which others might consider marginal at best. García Márquez converts the marginal into the central focus of this work, and remote geographical regions become the principal settings in which his human drama unfolds. He revitalizes forgotten segments of Colombian reality so that readers gain a more global perspective of this universe. His articles on El Chocó and other isolated areas of Colombia, whose most prominent features are the monumental neglect and oblivion in which they have existed for countless years, restore them to their proper place in the reality of the nation.

These texts clearly show García Márquez's vital interest in his native Colombia, and they contain paradigmatic elements which reappear in his fiction. These articles constitute early efforts to create a kind of fiction which John S. Brushwood characterizes as transcendent regionalism: "The transcendent regionalism present in many novels of the past quarter-century probes deeply into the character of a region. It is not photographic; it is not even a painting. It is a collage, or a happening, or both. It produces the experience of knowing a region intimately. The activity required by the experience makes the new, transcendent regionalism a more intimate experience than is possible in traditional regionalism of the oh-yes-I've-seen-that variety."[29] The move toward this new type of fiction coincides with the development of a spatial context which will enable García Márquez to "reinvent" the particular region with which he is dealing. The Chocó certainly offers him a challenge, since it is one of the most neglected and geographically isolated regions of Colombia.

The series on the Chocó, entitled "The Chocó Ignored by Colombia," appeared in four parts (September 29, 30 and October 1 and 2, 1954), and another article followed six months later called "The Chocó Unredeemed" (March 23, 1955). As Pedro Sorela explains, "one day *El Espectador* received a cablegram from its correspondent in Quibdó, the capital of the Department of the Chocó, in which he described an unprecedented demonstration of the Chocoans who were protesting against the government's proposal to divide up the Chocó among its neighboring departments. Similar cablegrams followed and García Márquez was sent to investigate 'what a city up in arms was like.'"[30] When García Márquez arrived, the city was deserted and there was no evidence of demonstrations. Finally, he found the correspondent Primo Guerrero: "He explained to me that no, there was nothing going on in Quibdó, but that he had believed that it was only right to send the protest cables. But since I had spent two days getting there, and the photographer was completely opposed to returning without any pictures, we decided, in complete agreement with Primo Guerrero, to organize a portable demonstration that was announced with drums and tambourines. On the second day, the information was sent out, and on the fourth day, an army of reporters and photographers arrived in search of the crowds of people. I had to explain to them that in this miserable town everybody was sleeping, but we organized a new and enormous protest, and that was how the Chocó was saved."[31] Therefore, although the story was not true, the author took advantage of the situation to denounce the horrible socioeconomic conditions of the region. To carry out his denunciation, the author uses various narrative strategies that reconfirm the bigeneric quality of his work.

In the first sentence, the author centers the reader's attention on its radical isolation: "Today it is still as difficult to get to Quibdó as it was 200 years ago. To found Quibdó again would today require as much work as two hundred years ago" (295). The best way to get there is the Atrato River, and the plane which lands in the river "looks like those expeditionary planes that searched for Tarzan" (295). The pilots of this plane "have the same intrepid spirit of the first settlers" (296). This reduction of the spatial context establishes the initial parameters in the reader's mind. The spatial contraction not only facilitates the reader's acceptance of its peculiar reality, but it naturalizes the text by appealing to the reader's preconceptions about the Chocó.

The author then negates the geographic reality surrounding the reduced spatial context: "On the map there is a road 160 kilometers long which is pure cartographic speculation: Medellín-Quibdó. To travel it is to suffer through an agonizing and exhausting 22-hour day in vehicles loaded with merchandise and animals" (296). The author openly declares his intention of "reinventing" the Chocó as a space: "For those reasons, travelling to the Chocó has been a slightly fantastic adventure for a century, and in addition, it is still an adventure waiting to be discovered" (296). As the subtitle, "The Unpublished Adventure," indicates, the narrator, who has already visited the region as a reporter, will now narrate the visit as a participant in the drama.

He thus creates a kind of double narrator which we can call a "narrator-silhouette," the narrator reliving the events as if they were happening again and the silhouette representing the "shadowy" presence of the first narrator. As Pedro Sorela says, this series "is a magical experience which is difficult to comprehend from a narrow and prosaic conception of journalism."[32] García Márquez transcends the limits of investigative reporting to rewrite the official reality of the Chocó and subject it to the dialogic interaction of the Chocoan voices. García Márquez, the reporter who originally visited the region, "shadows" his other narrator as the story unfolds again as a lived experience. This narrative strategy permits the author to recreate the Chocó as an adventure to be discovered.

The section entitled "A City in the Jungle" begins with a sentence focalized through the narrator-silhouette: "One has to know how to get to Quibdó in order to understand clearly what happened in the Chocó in recent weeks" (296). Although the time reference suggests a traditional subsequent time of narrating, the narration is focalized through a narrator who is visiting the region for the first time. Quibdó "looks like an encampment in the heart of the jungle," it has "dusty clapboard houses with zinc roofs," and "during business hours the population bakes in 100-degree temperatures in the shade" (296). Quibdó bears a certain resemblance to the future Macondo and other rural towns in García Márquez's fiction. He particularizes the town of Quibdó by saying that it does not resemble an African village. The reference is not gratuitous because the author does not wish his readers to make general comparisons which might detach Quibdó from its cultural context. In the following section, "The First Piece of News," the author again abandons his role as a journalist: "The departmental inspector, the man who shines shoes and the black woman who works in the hotel, give differently worded explanations, but they use the same arguments, because the Chocó has not progressed" (297). The extradiegetic-homodiegetic narrator (the reporter) becomes intradiegetic-homodiegetic (his silhouette) and narrates his own story, but in a very inconspicuous fashion.[33] When he reviews the reasons for the Chocó's lamentable state, it is as if he were there listening to the different people outline their explanations to him.

García Márquez exhibits more freedom in the Chocó series because he does not have to confront the same factual limitations of the articles on Medellín disaster in which the strict chronological ordering of events was essential. The article opens with a mixed analepsis concerning the links of the region to the outside world: "For many years, the Chocoans have been asking for a road. It doesn't matter in what direction the road goes, as long as it breaks the strangle hold of the jungle" (297).[34] This event relates to the continuous isolation of the region, whereas he relegates others to a minor role as external analepses: "However, 18 days ago, the professional announcer who reads the commercials over the loudspeaker system, told the citizens of Quibdó that, instead of the road for which they had been petitioning for so many years, the exact opposite was going to occur: the Chocó would be divided up and partitioned with one stroke of the pen" (297).[35] The news galvanizes the people into action, and the external analepsis serves to "unbottle" not the region but the pent up frustration of its inhabitants: "The whole population heard the news over the loudspeakers on the main street, and they stayed there for 13 days, singing, listening to speeches, waving the Colombian flag and the flag of Old Santa Marta, which is also the banner of the Chocó" (298). The reduction of the difference between the external analepsis and the narrative in the first degree to five days negates the durational importance of the event and intensifies the human participation in it.

In the section subtitled "Not a Single Incident," the reader glimpses the presence of the silhouette narrator: "Nevertheless, having gotten to know the Chocoans on their home ground, having lived among them and closely observed their movement, it is evident that the declaration of independence would probably never have materialized" (298). The absence of personal pronouns in the passage in Spanish prevents the reader from determining who perceives and who speaks, and the narrator and his silhouette counterpart seem to share the same focalization. The reader learns that "during the 400 hours of continuous demonstrations, not one complaint was uttered against Colombia or its government" (298). Although there were no demonstrations in Quibdó, this "fabrication" of the events is no less true than the official account which concealed other variants which the author's dialogical approach exposes and denounces. The double narrator creates a double-voiced discourse that continues to collect the "lost" voices of the inhabitants of the Chocó, even though they are not materially present in the narrative. The article now moves to within a day and a half of the narrative present, then rejoins it when the narrator refers to the only violent incident "which took place yesterday in the Chocó was a violent death in Carmen del Atrato, which was apparently caused by purely personal motives" (298).

The author introduces a series of completing homodiegetic internal analepses.[36] They fill in the paraleptic gap created earlier by the temporal reference of thirteen days, but from another perspective: the official world.[37] The reader also learns when the reporters from *El Espectador* arrived on the scene: "The president of the high court was giving his formal acceptance speech to the new governor while two blocks away some impromptu speakers, in front of a crowd of three thousand people, were greeting the group of reporters from *El Espectador* who were the first reporters to arrive in the Chocó. That same afternoon, after finishing 300 hours of continuous demonstrations, the crowd ran through the streets of the city, following the usual route" (299).

The governor to whom the author refers was a conservative who did not tolerate any form of criticism: "The situation in the Chocó was different from that of the rest of the country: Until September, 1954 the same governor remained in power who had been appointed by the Laureanist regime and he kept his job under the military dictatorship. His intolerance of the liberals led him to harass the local correspondents of *El Espectador* and *El Tiempo*, as if the new power structure would not have promised to put an end to the excesses of political sectarianism. That was how that 'godo' governor had the correspondent of *El Espectador* in Quibdó jailed twice in May and August of 1954."[38] If the demonstrations were a fabrication, the political ploys of the military government were pure prestidigitation and, in this case, it is perfectly legitimate to oppose one fiction with another, without violating journalistic norms. Indeed, as Jacques Gilard explains, "the political situation in the Chocó was denounced periodically on page 4 of *El Espectador* in Quibdó, in the editorial section as well as in the column called 'Day to Day.' The scandal provoked by the proposal to divide up the department had to be seized upon by the newspaper to mark another step in its confrontation with the military government."[39]

The narrator avoids mentioning whether he was one of the reporters from *El Espectador* who arrived at that moment, so that the scene is focalized through a person observing their arrival. The narrator has most likely been there for some time, at least eighteen days before the arrival of the reporters. Several temporal anachronies appear during the eighteen days from the announcement of the project to dismember the department to the completion of the 400 hours of continuous demonstration, which amounts to 16.6 days. The arrival of the journalists at the moment when 300 hours of demonstrations are completed coincides with the other reference to thirteen days (or 312 hours) of protests after the government's plan is made public. According to García Márquez, we already know that he and Primo Guerrero organized an impromptu demonstration and that two days after they sent out the news, a flood of reporters and photographers poured into the capital searching for the crowds of people. García Márquez shuffles time coordinates to highlight the intensity of Chocoan nationalism in the face of the failed policies of the military government. The mention of the 400 hours underscores the determination of the Chocoans and then he focuses on one moment (300 hours) to contrast the two political attitudes. The reference to the only violent incident which occurred the previous day returns the narrative to the present.

The dismemberment proposal is finally dropped, and the narrator adds this comment: "After all that, one has to believe that the declaration of independence by the Chocó would never have materialized, not even in the case of the department being divided up with a single stroke of a pen" (300). The remainder of the article deals with the disruption of the normal activities of those who devoted themselves to the cause of the Chocó. Despite all their hardships, "the facts have shown that they did not lose their lucidity and calm for a moment" (300). A song was composed for the occasion called *The Chocoan Lament*, and the narrator observes: "Seeing and hearing them, one remembered *The Cucaracha and Adelita* of the Mexican revolution" (301). Since no personal pronoun is used, it is not possible to pinpoint the focalizer. The use of the first person plural also blurs the identification of the narrator: "Those of us who attended those meetings have good reason to believe that the Chocoan people have the strength of spirit to have gone on resisting indefinitely" (301). In this article, then, García Márquez is not attempting to accumulate facts and data surrounding a series of events; rather he is interested in expanding the human context of the events and presenting them as lived experiences. Therefore, he employs a narrator-silhouette, a double yet combined narrative perspective which enables him to portray the Chocó in its daily, unfolding human context. García Márquez is thus able to transcend the events and show how people shape them.

In the second installment, subtitled "A Family United, Without Means of Communication," the author concentrates on the geographical bottleneck and isolation of the region: "It is difficult to get to Quibdó. But it is more difficult to leave" (302). Besides causing the Chocó's economic woes, this problem is also "the source of that ironclad unity and solid patriotism of the Chocoans" (302). In political terms, this unity transforms the region's inhabitants into a cohesive, extended family which could easily serve as an example for the rest of the country: "The alarming thing is that the nation, throughout its history, has not helped in any real way to stimulate, through adequate means of communication, that Chocoan unity that can be so useful and exemplary for the rest of the country" (303). This indirect comment corresponds to García Márquez's conception of politics;

that is, the division, sharing and exercise of power by different segments of society without any idea of strict hierarchization.

The unity of the Chocoans stems from their opposition to a legal system that isolates, marginalizes and prevents them from gaining access to the free market. Confronted with the government's grandiose development plans, whose economic policies favor the foreign companies and a small class of rich oligarchs, the Chocoans have to create their own extralegal system to be able to live and overcome their obstacles. The legal system denies them the opportunity to produce freely, and the government is mainly concerned with redistributing the existing national wealth among the groups who are already well positioned to take advantage of the legal system to protect themselves against free economic competition, instead of promoting those economic activities that will generate more economic wealth. In the Chocó, like many other marginalized regions, an informal economy develops on the periphery of the legal system. Moreover, the informal economy represents a powerful force that often produces more economic wealth than the legal, formal economy. However, the government, determined to redistribute and not to promote and facilitate free competition, has not been able to tap this source. These governments are based on the antediluvian ideas of mercantilist intervention in the economic sector. While governments establish an enormous bureaucratic apparatus to control the economic activities, the individual entrepreneurs, instead of engaging in a free market economy, waste their time and energy on useless efforts trying to surmount the legal obstacles. The large majority of entrepreneurs, excluded legally from the open market, work in the informal economy which is regulated by an extralegal system. The informal entrepreneurs devote so much time and energy to protecting their businesses that their production is very minimal. They are not going to invest much time and money in the expansion of their business ventures because they are not legal. The informals always work under the threat of the same legal system which should be protecting them in the open market.

There seem to exist societal enclaves where self-determination is still possible, but people, not governments, will convert this possibility into reality. Isolation has a salutary effect because when the inhabitants are aware not only of their isolation, but also of the validity of their self-generated and self-regulated socioeconomic system, they can then function as a unit. García Márquez always challenges the presumed benefits of intervention in the name of progress, and he believes that these societal enclaves have to establish an internal pattern of development. Progress can be as illusory as the road maps of the Chocó: "The stretch of road from Quibdó to Yuto appears in outlined form on maps. That is another cartographic speculation. Not even a tree has been cut down to explore the area" (303). Evidently, the road will never be built unless it serves the interests of the small, empowered groups who already possess wealth and do not produce anything. To them the Chocó is a region to be exploited, whereas for García Márquez, it is to be explored, and therein lies one of the fundamental differences between the two perspectives on the Chocó.

Reality in the Chocó coincides very closely with García Márquez's own conception: "Contrary to what has always happened, in the Chocó it is the towns which must inevitably pass through the roads and not the roads through the towns" (305). Reality simply does not follow any prescribed pattern in the Chocó, which constitutes a "great administrative paradox" (305). The sociopolitical reality of the Chocó contradicts the absurd legal system that relegates the region to oblivion, and produces preposterous situations worthy of magical realism. García Márquez does not have to invent anything to discover magical realism in the Chocó. The town of Cértegui "was left without a road because the construction engineer would take baths in the nude in town and the police inspector called it to his attention. The engineer retaliated by leaving Cértegui without a road" (305). There is "a bust of General Uribe that somehow survived the period of violence" and a certain Donaldo Lozano "assures that three weeks ago he turned on the faucet in his house and out came the skin of a snake" (306), and because the plane did not deliver the regular supply of national cigarettes, "everyone in Istmina must be smoking foreign cigarettes, which must already be much cheaper than the national brand" (306).

The impossible conditions created by the lack of roads has resulted in a situation very close to García Márquez's understanding of reality, one full of contradictory, human, and surprising elements: "If it is difficult to travel to the Chocó from anywhere in the country, it is more difficult to travel in the Chocó" (307). Quibdó is separated from the port of Bahía Solano by one hundred kilometers, but people refer to it as some kind of legendary place because it is so difficult to get there. In addition, "the towns of the Pacific coast are isolated from one another. Bahía Solano is unaware of how the oranges of Cúpica taste, in spite of the fact that they are only an inch apart on the map" (308). The Chocó thus offers a panoply of characteristics which García Márquez will reincorporate into his fictional world without, as he often repeats, inventing anything. All these are products of the economic model that is used to "develop" these isolated regions. It is based on the government's legal involvement in the extractive economy and its dependence on foreign companies. A road or a railroad will only be built to exploit the natural resources of these regions, and no effort is made to promote the free market economy in which everyone can participate and compete.

The third article continues to portray the Chocó within the framework of the magical realism. The first subheading introduces the reader to this particular reality: "Here people learn how to read in the civil code" (312). People learn to read in the civil code because it contains all the absurd laws which imprison the inhabitants of the Chocó. Amazingly, this reality springs from the most remote places like Samurindo where life is a constant struggle against the impenetrable jungle: "Everyone knows how to read and write, and can explain any problem of the Chocó, without being asked, simply because of the habit of repeating it every day" (312). The department's problems have been ignored for so long, and so many promises have been made and broken, that discussion of these problems has become a reflex action. Even though the inhabitants of the region exhibit a high degree of political unity, the country neither takes advantage of it nor possesses anything like it on a national scale. We see to what extent magical realism, political protest and economic questions can combine in the author's writing. The government will never promote national unity within the legal framework to unleash the productive energies of all its inhabitants as long as its primary goals are to stay in power and redistribute the national wealth among its cronies. The case of the Chocó, multiplied many times, corroborates the failure and futility of this system. In reality, the only remote place is the very government which excludes the majority of the country from the economic pie.

History is also a vital part of living reality, and if someone asks where Balboa discovered the Pacific, "they will tell him that the discovery was made in a place in the Chocó where a law was issued by General Uribe Uribe for an obelisk which was never erected" (312). History is absorbed and refracted throughout the different social strata so that it supports the socioeconomic system of the Chocó. García Márquez obviously admires this region which must create its own political realities: "That development of a region which knows it is capable, which prides itself on understanding its problems completely and believes that it does not let itself be fooled, although it has been deceived many times, is the result of having learned for centuries in school that the Chocó is an important entity, special and indivisible, but completely forgotten by the nation" (313-14).

In some respects, the Chocoans enjoy more freedom than many other people, and the author illustrates this point in his depiction of Condoto, which is "a town with twisting streets, with large wooden houses, a sad and desolate town, but not a miserable town" (315). In many ways it resembles Macondo, especially regarding its links to a more glorious past of which only nostalgic vestiges remain. Macondo bathes in nostalgia to the end, but Condoto refuses to be engulfed. Its past is directly linked to an economic boom and bust cycle similar to Macondo's: "The Russians, the Swedish, the Chinese, all the desperate remnants of humanity swept along and deposited there by the platinum whirlwind, passed beneath the glowing candelabra of those houses in which bank notes were burned, like in the Banana Zone, and today you cannot dance inside them for fear that they will collapse" (315).

The inhabitants of Condoto, "tied to their memories of a past whose complete destruction they cannot understand, have not let themselves be swept away by misery" (315). The town struggles silently and ferociously against the nostalgia trap, while its poverty and suffering stare it in the face: "There the past did not ebb away silently, as in other areas. It was carried by a strong, dark wind of fate" (316). The past stubbornly clings to the present because economic exploitation has continued unabated, and has left the region on the sidelines: "But deep down they are thinking about platinum. They cannot understand that right there, in the backyards of their houses, a dredger is removing enormous amounts of earth, uncovering the riches of the river bed while they sit down at a table which in 1918 was decorated with gold engravings and which is now used to eat a little plain rice and three slices of cold plantain" (316). The wide disparity between the economic development of the Chocó and the nostalgic wealth of its inhabitants constitutes yet another indictment of the legal system which excludes much more than it includes. In many ways, magical realism bases itself on the hard economic and legal reality which has created the other reality in which the Chocoans live. One of the major problems plaguing the region is the persistent economic nostalgia which imprisons the people from generation to generation: "The children learn about that legendary past in school. But when the teacher tells it, they already know it. They learned it at home at meal times, when they got up and when they went to bed" (316). This self-deception will have tragic consequences for Macondo, and the author remarks that it is necessary to focus on teaching agriculture because the recovery of the metallic past is a sterile illusion.

García Márquez returns to one of his familiar themes in this article: the phenomenon of the economic boom, its inequities and

the continuous debate concerning the value of progress.   The
subheading leaves little doubt about the author's attitude: "The
Useless Wealth of Colombian Platinum."   In the middle of the
jungle, the company town stands in stark contrast to Andagoyita:
"It is called Andagoya, located between San Juan and Condoto,
and it has electric lights, an aqueduct, a perfectly good telephone
service, boat docks, and launches that belong to the same city, and
shady and beautiful tree-lined streets.   The small, clean houses,
with spacious fenced areas and picturesque wooden steps to the
porches, seemed to be planted in the thick clean lawn.   Inside you
breathe a healthy and refreshing air, and the kitchen, equipped with
all the modern conveniences, like the dining room, pantry and the
bedrooms, is as neat and silent as the rest of the house" (318).
This new city is inhabited by people from all over the world,
including "Colombians who have forgotten the nostalgia and are
better off there than in the capital of the republic" (319).   The city
bears the same name of the conquistador who discovered Panama,
which was formerly part of Colombia.[40]   Andagoya is an instant
replay of the old economic policy of the extractive economy:
"Andagoya is a young city: it cannot be over 50 years.   It was
founded, enlarged and is governed by an American mining company
which no one in the country has talked about for a long time: the
Chocó Pacífico" (319).   This modern, well-organized city is the
opposite of its native counterpart, Andagoyita, which is "built with
the human waste products and left over material from Andagoya"
(319).   The miserable and sad town "is almost entirely made up of
prostitutes" (319).   In Andagoyita, the prostitutes and workers live
in squalor and misery, and no attempt has been made to improve
the living conditions for these people.

It is evident that nothing has changed since the company first
started to operate in the region.   Low wages, substandard housing,
the lack of medical care and the absence of tangible economic
benefits, offer a paradigmatic image of a situation repeated
throughout Latin America.   All that remains for the inhabitants is
the bitter pill of nostalgia, but their situation has not improved at
all.   It is a closed, self-sustaining economic system which functions
within very strict boundaries: "For thirty years the mining company

has been operating its own hydroelectric plant which provides energy to all the towns in the area. The company built a private road which skirts Condoto two kilometers away from it. The company navigates the rivers on its huge dredgers extracting gold and platinum, and ruining the soil along the shore with the dredgings" (321). This situation has led to a muted rebellion on the part of the region's inhabitants: "It is very likely that that feeling of injustice, nurtured for many years, developed through a harsh and somewhat somber desperation, is a determining factor in that certain exaggerated quality of the inhabitants of Condoto" (322).

The author centers on the problem of electricity which the company supplies or cuts off at will to the surrounding villages, and the opposition of the inhabitants to their monopoly: "The struggle is tenacious, constant and has given rise to an atmosphere of unbearable tension" (322). The author does not offer a definitive solution, for he is viewing a situation in which an outside force has been operating for a long time. Although the Chocó and its inhabitants possess many admirable qualities, they find themselves in a seemingly inextricable situation, torn between their nostalgia for the past and the outside economic forces which marginalize them in their own native land.

Six months later García Márquez wrote another article, "The Chocó Unredeemed" (March 23, 1955), in which he directly confronted the government of Rojas Pinilla and his political prestidigitation. The repetition of time adverbs exposes the complete emptiness of this policy: "At the present time, six months have passed since the speech at Carmen de Bolívar. Six months since the president offered to visit the Chocó. Six months since the promise was given to construct a road system in the most isolated department in the country. And six months since a political pact between the two parties was signed during a solemn ceremony held in the public square in the city of Quibdó."[41] Then comes the reality: "Six months have passed and the first stone has still not been put in place. The president of the republic has not visited the Chocó, nor has he made any decision concerning the political pact signed by the leaders of both parties on September

23" (543). The government's inaction shows how the policies of mercantilist governments seek to control and redistribute the national wealth. In another act of political illusionism, the government decentralizes its authority: "Recently, the office in charge of carrying out municipal development projects was eliminated, and its functions were transferred to the office in Medellín" (543). If the government really wanted to decentralize its authority, it would empower the municipal authorities to make decisions without government intervention.

This policy of neglect also forces the excluded to search for alternative solutions to their economic problems in order to counteract the controls imposed by the government: "Business taxes have skyrocketed, and the departmental and municipal authorities can find no other solution to meet the needs of public services. The rural inhabitants of the Chocó are emigrating towards Panama" (543). To synthesize and crystallize the result of this policy, the author offers a Gestalt image of the settlement of Juradó which the sea is erasing from the map: "Right now, it is highly likely that no one in Colombia in the next twenty-four hours can say for sure whether Juradó still exists, or if three months ago it was wiped off the map by the invasion of the sea" (544). He again indicts the government and its redistributive system because the Chocó "is a department with influential men who have held prestigious national positions in all the governments, but nevertheless the department has needed a large scale program of public works for twenty-six years and it has never been started" (544). Obviously, these influential men have never enjoyed the favor of the successive governments because the Chocó has never received any of the redistributed national wealth.

This series on the Chocó constitutes another step in the continuous process, initiated in the first reportage on the tragedy of Antioquia, of the indirect subversion that will lead to the most serious confrontation with the official world in another long account published in *El Espectador*, *The Story of the Shipwrecked Sailor*. García Márquez was probably aware of this process, and in the next series about the Colombian veterans who returned from fighting in the Korean war, he undermines the official patriotism by exposing the outrageous neglect and mistreatment of the veterans. Moreover, these reportages enable him to develop a method of oblique subversion through narrative discourse that surpasses the limitations of orthodox investigative reporting. The working conditions of *El Espectador* supported and encouraged this method, and García Márquez took full advantage of the sudden expansion of the journalistic space to perfect his bigeneric writing.

Journalism, Opposition and Political Discourse

García Márquez's investigative reporting also brought him into contact with political and social issues in Colombia and with the power structure of the official world which shapes the events. García Márquez works within the human context which simultaneously produces and experiences these events. His journalism never constitutes an official record of events; rather it is a human chronicle of official history, a deep probing of the polyphonic resonances which human events engender.

The political ideas of García Márquez, the official position of *El Espectador* as an opposition newspaper to the dictatorship of Rojas Pinilla and the journalistic method of the author, would put him on a collision course with the centers of power. Power has always fascinated García Márquez, and the stages that we have examined in these longer series suggest that he is trying to reach the center of power from which he can observe it functioning and then subvert it through narrative discourse. This position signifies that García Márquez frequently surpasses the orthodox limits and definitions of journalism. As Pedro Sorela aptly points out: "In any case, every attempt to 'classify' García Márquez as a reporter is necessarily incomplete, and it would be an error to try to 'fit' him into a predetermined category."[42] Each long journalistic piece, starting with the Antioquia story, represents a "refrito" of an already narrated and classified reality, but the ostensible solidity of the official version reveals its vulnerability because it is based on the proairetic code which establishes the linear sequentiality of the events and on the monoglottic voice of authority. García Márquez realizes that the "refrito" contains the multitude of voices which have been temporarily suppressed by the unitary voice of authority. The chief aim of García Márquez's reportages is the manumission of the vocal polyphony that surrounds every event, and this liberation will necessarily generate different versions of an event. The author is not concerned with producing another account of the event because he does not want to commit the same error of repressing the manifold human voices.

A more "complete" version could be constructed by comparing all the variants, but the events would still overshadow the human context. The version is also a prevalent journalistic technique: "The version is a piece of information or a series of facts which have a minimal basis in reality, and which are linked to the behavior of one or several sources and also to the deductive and inductive processes of the journalist."[43] The version "involves probability, taking into account the arguments on which it is based."[44] The version is based on the declarations of witnesses who express different points of view about the same object. In reality, journalistic objectivity is an illusion which is embedded in the immediacy of reported facts. Even in the live coverage of an event (also called a running commentary), in which the commentary follows the action so closely that they can almost be considered simultaneous, objectivity proves illusory because another commentator or witness would still present a slightly different account. García Márquez not only prefers already narrated stories but he also chooses those events which he himself did not witness. This preference can seem highly paradoxical in a profession where the journalist is a contemporary who looks for closure and finality, since the news story, unlike history, is born and dies in a short space of time. García Márquez prefers to expand the human context of the news story and he realizes that the purely journalistic treatment of an event cannot go too far beyond the proairetic code and, in many cases, the human context and the multivocality of the event are lost. Regarding the propagandistic discourse of the dictatorship, his reportages attempt to undermine it by freeing the voices contained in the "refritos. In the series on the veterans who returned from the Korean War, "an unspoken opposition to Colombian participation in the Korean War runs through the whole story, a participation condemned, among others, but principally, by the Communist Party."[45]

In "From Korea to Reality" (December 9, 10 and 11, 1954), García Márquez opposes the official, patriotic welcome created by the government in order to reveal the pariah status that greeted many veterans upon returning home. He exposes the fraudulent stance of the official world and decries the futility of war. He also criticizes the United States for helping to create the false ideas about the war: "When the news about the recruitment became known, many of the present veterans say that there was a rumor going around that when the volunteers returned from Korea, they would receive special scholarships, life pensions and the means to live in the United States" (403). The author uses rumor to show the falsity of the official reality. Rumor "is a specific proposal to believe something which passes from one person to another, usually in oral form, and without any sure way of proving it."[46] In journalism rumor "is a piece of information which the journalist picks up in the social sphere, but the fact that it does not come a reliable source prevents him from considering it very seriously."[47] The fact that rumor emanates from unreliable sources indicates that the regime of Rojas Pinilla, through its propaganda machine, circulated a series of rumors among the soldiers who would continue to delude themselves as they repeated them.

The official world entices and captures its victims with ceremony and empty promises. The Colombian contingent is greeted by the South Korean president, Singman Rhee, who probably for the first time in his life "officially said the name of that faraway and unknown South American country which was sending 1,063 men to his country in order to fight against the Communists" (403). The author expresses his deep suspicion of official history: "The historians surely found a good literary device in order to write the history of the Korean War" (403); that is, it will be a purely fictional account of what really happened. For García Márquez, the real story belongs to the veterans who lived through it: "But that story is much more interesting and human as told by the privates"

(403). The author centers on the privates because in spite of having a voice, they do not have the right to act for themselves. They have fought in Korea and obeyed the orders of the military hierarchy, and once back in Colombia, the government tries to stifle their voices. García Márquez continues to recover these anonymous voices to reinstate their human value and to denounce the false promises and the propaganda of the government.

García Márquez searches for the human context in his writing, and his reliance on official sources is always counterbalanced by his trust in human sources. He draws his material from the soldiers of the lowest rank because they participated most directly in the conflict. At first, it seemed like a phony war, "a continuous training program, with all the conveniences that they didn't have at home, during the first three months of preparation" (404). After their first taste of real battle and death, the masters of illusion take over: "Nevertheless, in spite of the danger and the feeling of being only one step ahead of death, there was something unexpected in this war which the soldiers from Colombia weren't used to. By itself, breakfast, prepared in accordance with the American diet, was better than many of the lunches that the soldiers would eat every day in Colombia, with money they made honestly" (405). Since Colombia was the only Latin American country to send troops to Korea, and since United States military aid was helping to bring the Colombian military back into the political arena, García Márquez undoubtedly links the acts of prestidigitation to the U.S.

His critique comes across in an indirect fashion: "The soldiers from Colombia, who looked small fighting alongside the robust Americans, understood then for the first time how important it was to shoot first" (405). The Colombians are fighting a war which has no benefits for them, which they do not understand, but the official world offers them continued enticements: "General James A. Van Vleet, commander of the Eighth Army, sent them a special message of congratulations for their outstanding fighting in the Kumsong offensive" (405). The author points an accusing finger at the U.S.: "The American invasion made the R & R business prosper in Japan. The Korean War reinforced its splendor" (406). The war throws things out of focus, and the Colombian soldiers become not only war casualties, but victims of an illusion: "It is very likely that no poor or rich Colombian has felt as embarrassingly rich as the Colombian soldiers in Japan" (406). This stands in sharp contrast to the economic situation which awaits them when they return home. The soldiers enjoyed the transitory fruits of their stay in Korea, which García Márquez enumerates in a series of sentences starting with "They learned that." When the soldiers return to Colombia, the official world divests them of their illusions, leaving them with "two pants pockets in which to put their hands" (407). The soldiers are then portrayed as social misfits in their own society, and stories circulate about their unstable mental condition. The rumor mill of propagandistic discourse now fabricates rumors to discredit the same soldiers that the first rumors had falsely praised. Obviously, the government's only concern is to maintain the facade of patriotism and its own legitimacy in the public eye. If necessary, the government will deceive everyone to stay in power.

In the second installment, subtitled "The Hero Who Pawned His Medals," García Márquez focuses on the human context in order to depict the reality of the situation. As can be expected, the returning veterans were "convinced that their veteran's status would open the door to good paying jobs" (408). Instead, these veterans found only closed doors, and public attention centered on the criminal activities. Two cases in particular confirmed "the incorrect theory that absolutely all the Korean veterans are dangerous individuals, due to the mental disorders that the war produced in them" (409). García Márquez tries to rectify this situation by demonstrating that the veterans have more often been victims of violence than its actual perpetrators. He presents a rapid series of cases which constitute a Gestalt image of the veterans' plight, and the image of victimization crystallizes in Angel Fabio Goes, "who had lost an eye and one hand in the war, and was stabbed in an ambush in Cañasgordas, by three unidentified men who escaped from justice" (410). These cases create the image of the widespread violence carried out against the veterans, and the statement from one dying veteran carries an implicit accusation of government complicity: "They didn't kill me in Korea, and now they end up killing me in Bogotá" (410). The veterans' personal accounts act as a powerful indictment of the official world, and the reader easily completes the picture of the violence.

In this feature story, García Márquez takes a more openly political stance anchored in the human context. At the time of the Korean War, Colombia was undergoing the bloody spasms of the "Violence." The Korean War offered a convenient way for the civilian government to rid itself of some of the unruly military officers and to offer "employment opportunites" to the young men who could not find work in the private sector. García Márquez recognizes the ploy and says flatly: "Between the battlefields of Colombia and the embattled cities of Colombia, in which the simple, ordinary attempt to get a job was like trying to wage war, many preferred the battlefields of Korea" (411). False promises undoubtedly contributed to convincing people to volunteer, especially those who really had no other option. Those who suffered the most were, as always, the campesinos whom the Violence had already deeply affected. The author epitomizes the cruel fate of the veterans in a bitter synecdochal image: "On November 26, 2,000 pounds of the remains of Colombian soldiers arrived in Buenaventura. The remains of men from all over Colombia, turned into ashes and put in special urns, were arriving there" (411). He adds a note of human tragedy by singling out "the mother of one of them, an old black woman, [who] lives by herself in Quibdó, in poverty and supported by public charity" (411). After highlighting the lamentable state of the wounded veterans, the author concludes this article with an ironic restatement of an earlier sentence: "It is thus a very human thing for a hero to pawn his medals" (412), and this is especially true considering the economic plight of the veterans.

In the final segment, subtitled "Every Veteran, a Solitary Problem," the author attacks the spurious logic which converts the veterans into a group of mental misfits. The term "veteran" applies to everyone who served in Korea, so that many who never saw combat are also classified as pariahs. The facts presented by the author not only counteract this negative image, but also expose the inhuman treatment of the veterans whose usefulness to the official world has terminated. Not only do many veterans who were treated for emotional problems hold jobs, but many noncombatants cannot find work, and finally, "to emphasize an important point, it must be said that not a single Korean veteran is confined in Sibate" (414). The author appeals to his readers' emotions, and statistics, numbers, and other forms of official data will not achieve the goal he is seeking.

The reasons for the veterans' inability to reintegrate themselves into society lie in the destabilizing sociopolitical climate of Colombia which existed before the men went to Korea: "That would be exactly what happened to the young man who was chased out of his village in 1948 by the political violence and who in 1951 answered the army's call for volunteers because he had spent three years in the city as an outcast where he found safety but in return he didn't find any work" (415). While admitting the possibility that a certain psychopathic personality would induce some men to enlist, García Márquez maintains his antigovernment stance on this issue: "What is missing is a true interest in their situation; an interest which has never really existed anywhere in the country, perhaps because it's been thought that the solution is much more complicated than it may actually be" (416). García Márquez uses journalistic objectivity to indict certain official segments of Colombian society which have conducted a campaign of gossip mongering to create a pariah image of a group of men who served as a political expedient. This series marks García Márquez entry into the larger arena of national politics, and this trend will continue in several other articles.

Conclusion: To Literature and Journalism Bound

The reportages of García Márquez derive from official versions whose events have already entered into their linear sequentiality and have been classified and anointed by the authorities. His articles revitalize these accounts by freeing them from the prison house of official language. In contrast to the journalist who tries to find definitive answers, García Márquez always subjects the sacred facts of journalism to dialogic interaction so that they come into direct contact with the voices of the human ambience which continuously produces the events. García Márquez's method differs from the idea of journalism which was prevalent at that time: "Anyone who knows the inside workings of a news agency knows that one of the methods used to express 'opinion' is the abundant information about an event, or its silencing. This idea of journalism as a an objective account of the events, using standard techniques, without any input by the journalist, is what with the passage of time 'dissident' journalists started to call disparagingly 'stenographic journalism,' thereby suggesting that the journalist does not develop his story, but limits himself to a photographic reproduction of reality."[48] On the contrary, García Márquez, throughout his career, "has given evidence of having a special interest in the idea of 'narrative' journalism, that is, with more room for input and participation by the journalist."[49] The "refritos" of the events afford him the opportunity to resuscitate the moribund reality of facts without restricting himself to presenting another official version.

García Márquez certainly documents and investigates the facts, but he always tries to overcome the documentary barrier to show their multidimensional reality, to break the silence which they impose. According to Pedro Sorela, García Márquez was already working in the context of new journalism which requires, among other things, "an authentic talent on the part of the writer and also the adoption of a point of view which discards objectivity."[50] In new journalism the writer also amasses many details, but they serve to create a certain atmosphere. García Márquez "works fundamentally within the context of 'advocacy journalism' in which the journalist takes a stance in favor of one side or the other in his story."[51] The author's involvement in his articles assumes a narrative form, and his writing proves most effective when he deals with official "refritos." García Márquez's journalism exposes events to the dialogic forces which modify, distort and change the same events. In this context, his journalism is necessarily subversive because, ultimately, he contradicts and opposes the official version.

In the three reportages that we have examined, García Márquez seems to have consciously guided the propagandistic discourse of the government towards a direct confrontation which would crystallize in his longest series on the sailor Luis Alejandro Velasco. The subversion of García Márquez always aims directly at the *how an event occurred* and never *what happened*. If García Márquez violates the traditional standards of objective, reportorial journalism, it is because the naked facts conceal much more than they reveal. Behind the *what happened* lies a whole human context which produced the event, and this is what he searches for in his news stories. The facts and events cannot be detached from their human context without losing their meaning. The facts only take on meaning in their human context, and the recovery of the human element is perhaps the most important goal of his journalism. Therefore, from his first text García Márquez undertakes the exploration of the vast field of the hypertextual relations of the Infinite Text which contributes to his bigeneric work, and this project is grounded in narrative productivity. If it is true that we all want to find out what is happening, that all of us share the desire to hear the news, García Márquez recognizes that there are many ways to know, understand and apprehend reality, and since he is always surprised by reality, narrative discourse provides him with the best way to know. Human beings produce events and journalism, among other mass media, transmits these events, but all too often the facts suppress the voices and shroud the human content. Freeing the voices is a subversive act in itself, especially when it involves governments and other official institutions which want to establish and impose a monolithic concept of reality. In this struggle to liberate the human context, *The Story of a Shipwrecked Sailor* represents the most perilous encounter with power and the official world.

Notes

1.   Gabriel García Márquez, *Obra periodística, Vol. 2: Entre cachacos I,* ed. Jacques Gilard (Barcelona: Bruguera, 1982), 7-8. Translation is mine.

2.   Pedro Sorela, *El otro García Márquez: Los años difíciles* (Madrid: Mondadori, 1988), 72. All translations are mine.

3.   Pedro Sorela, 72-3.

4.   Sorela, 73.

5.   Sorela, 74.

6.   Sorela, 74.

7.   Sorela, 75.

8.   Sorela, 78.

9.   Stephen Minta, *García Márquez: Writer of Colombia* (New York: Harper & Row, 1987), 41.

10.   Jacques Gilard, "La obra periodística de García Márquez, 1954-1956," *Revista de crítica literaria latinoamericana* (Lima), 2.4 (July/December, 1976), 151. All translations are mine.

11.   Gilard, *La obra periodística*, 153.

12.   "Just as it would be difficult to overemphasize Ortega's impact on Latin America, it would be difficult to do the same with Spengler's. *The Decline of the West* appeared in Manuel García Morente's masterful translation (done with the assistance of Ortega himself) in 1923. It was an immediate best-seller whose impact on Latin America was instantaneous and pervasive." Roberto González Echevarría, *Alejo Carpentier: The Pilgrim at Home* (Ithaca: Cornell UP, 1977), 54-5.

13. Oswald Spengler, *The Decline of the West*, 2 Vols., trans. Charles Francis Atkinson (New York: Alfred A. Knopf, 1983), 1: 107.

14. Roberto González Echevarría, *Alejo Carpentier*, 56.

15. Gilard, *La obra periodística*, 154.

16. Ronald Weber, *The Literature of Fact: Literary Nonfiction in American Writing* (Athens: Ohio UP, 1980), 2.

17. Ronald Weber, *The Literature of Fact*, 2.

18. Weber, *The Literature of Fact*, 2.

19. Weber, 45.

20. Weber, 47.

21. Weber, 48-9.

22. Pedro Sorela, *El otro García Márquez*, 78.

23. Jacques Gilard, "La obra periodística de García Márquez, 1954-1956," 155.

24. Gabriel García Márquez, *Obra periodística, Vol. 2: Entre cachacos I*, ed. Jacques Gilard (Barcelona: Editorial Bruguera, 1982), 245. All subsequent quotes will come from this edition and page numbers will be given in parentheses. All translations are mine unless otherwise indicated.

25. Alexis Márquez Rodríguez, *La comunicación impresa: Teoría y práctica del lenguaje periodístico* (Caracas: Ediciones Centauro, 1976), 123. Translations are mine.

26. Roland Barthes, *S/Z*, trans. Richard Miller (New York: Hill and Wang, 1974), 85.

27. Márquez Rodríguez, 124.

28. Márquez Rodríguez, 129.

29. John S. Brushwood, *The Spanish American Novel: A Twentieth-Century Survey* (Austin: University of Texas Press, 1975), 335.

30. Pedro Sorela, *El otro García Márquez*, 134-35.

31. Sorela, 135.

32. Sorela, 134.

33. Gérard Genette defines the extradiegetic-homodiegetic narrator as a narrator "in the first degree who tells his own story" and the intradiegetic-homodiegetic narrator as one "in the second degree who tells his own story." *Narrative Discourse: An Essay in Method*, trans. Jane E. Lewin (Ithaca: Cornell UP, 1983), 248.

34. Mixed analepses are those "whose reach goes back to a point earlier and whose extent arrives at a point later than the beginning of the first narrative." Gérard Genette, *Narrative Discourse*, 49.

35. In an external analepsis, its "entire extent remains external to the extent of the first narrative." Gérard Genette, *Narrative Discourse*, 49.

36. Homodiegetic internal analepses are "internal analepses that deal with the same line of action as the first narrative." These analepses are "completing" when they comprise "the retrospective sections that fill in, after the event, an earlier gap in the narrative." Gérard Genette, *Narrative Discourse*, 51.

37. Paralepsis involves "taking up and giving information which should be left aside." Gérard Genette, *Narrative Discourse*, 195.

38. Gabriel García Márquez, *Obra periodística Vol. 2: Entre cachacos I*, 73-74.

39. Jacques Gilard, *Entre cachacos I*, 74.

40. Pascual de Andagoya, 1495-1548, was a Spanish conquistador and one of the founders of Panama. Panama became an independent country on November 3, 1903.

41. Gabriel García Márquez, *Obra periodística Vol. 3: Entre cachacos II*, ed. Jacques Gilard (Barcelona: Bruguera, 1982), 541-42. Translation is mine. All other references will be given in the text with page numbers in parentheses.

42. Pedro Sorela, *El otro García Márquez*, 136.

43. Raúl Rivadeneira Prada, *Periodismo: La teoría de los sistemas y la ciencia de la comunicación* (México: Editorial Trillas, 1977), 79. Translation is mine.

44. Raúl Rivadeneira Prada, *Periodismo*, 79. Translation is mine.

45. Pedro Sorela, *El otro García Márquez*, 137.

46. Rivadeneira Prada, *Periodismo*, 76-7.

47. Rivadeneira Prada, 78.

48. Pedro Sorela, *El otro García Márquez*, 147-8.

49. Sorela, 148.

50. Sorela, 149.

51. Sorela, 149.

Chapter 5

Gestalt Imagining, Double Narrator, Focalization And the Dualist Power Position of García Márquez in *The Story of a Shipwrecked Sailor*

From the inception of the hyphenated writing career of García Márquez in 1947, we encounter a series of confrontations with the official world and its versions of the historical events. His three reportages for *El Espectador* trace a direct path to his spectacular feature story on the accident of the destroyer *ARC Caldas* in which eight sailors were washed overboard and disappeared. The only survivor, Luis Alejandro Velasco, spent ten days adrift in a life raft before reaching the Atlantic coast of Colombia (this series was published in fourteen parts in 1955 in *El Espectador* and then as a book in 1970 with the title *The Story of a Shipwrecked Sailor*).[1]

Throughout his career, García Márquez has endeavored to penetrate the inner circles of power, and this quest is accompanied by a continuous fascination and obsession with the phenomenon of power and his concomitant effort to undermine it through narrative discourse: "I was less interested in the figure of the feudal dictator as such than in the opportunity to reflect on the nature of power. This is an underlying theme running through all my books. Because I've always thought absolute power is the highest and most complex of human achievements and, therefore, it is the essence of man's nobility and of his degradation. As Lord Acton said, 'All power corrupts and absolute power corrupts absolutely.' This has to be an enthralling subject for a writer."[2] One of the forms that power assumes is the official history which offers itself as the only authentic version of the facts. García Márquez fully realizes the futility of producing another historical variant because it will end up reconfirming and resolidifying the official version.

García Márquez utilizes another strategy to breach and subvert the ostensible solidity of historical events: he assimilates the historical events to the fictional universe, transfers them to a

161

double narrator (a retrospective narrator and a character-narrator), and then undermines the events through narrative discourse. This approach also enables him to safeguard his dualist power position. García Márquez also succeeds in creating a Gestalt image of the accident which enables the reader to supply the missing details while participating in the subversive act that García Márquez carries out.

The reportage on the perilous adventure of the sailor Luis Alejandro Velasco marks a decisive turning point in the treatment of focalization: García Márquez creates a tripartite perspective which integrates the retrospective narrator, the character-narrator and the reader. This change signals the retrospective narrator's almost total abandonment of the prerogatives of zero focalization or what is traditionally called omniscience. The rejection of zero focalization coincides with the subversive act that the author carried out at the moment the official world was trying to cover up the real circumstances surrounding the accident. Omniscience constitutes an illusory and false concept because the author has nothing to "know," since he invents everything. It is more accurate to talk about the *totality of information* and its restriction by the author. In *The Story of a Shipwrecked Sailor*, although the narrators focalize from different perspectives, the separation is so negligible that the reader does not have to vacillate constantly between them, trying to decide who perceives and who speaks. Essentially, the reader finally adopts the same focalization as the other narrative participants.

In the preface to the 1970 edition, García Márquez describes the intense work involved in producing Velasco's account: "In twenty daily sessions, each lasting six hours, during which I took notes and sprang trick questions on him to expose contradictions, we put together an accurate and concise account of his ten days at sea. Not solely for that reason but also because it seemed fitting, we agreed that the story would be written in the first person and signed by him. This is the first time my name has appeared in connection with the text."[3] Although García Márquez downplays his role in the production of the text, the use of the first person suits his narrative strategy in this series. Moreover, García Márquez's ideas about interviews and his subsequent remarks about the genesis of *The Story of a Shipwrecked Sailor* confirm his major role in producing this text:

> As for me, I sincerely believe that interviewing is a kind of fictional genre and that it must be regarded in this light. The majority of journalists let the tape recorder do the work, and they think that they are respecting the wishes of the person they are interviewing by retranscribing word for word what he says. They do not realize that this work method is really quite disrespectful: whenever someone speaks, he hesitates, goes off on tangents, does not finish his sentences, and he makes trifling remarks. For me the tape recorder must only be used to record material that the journalist will decide to use later on, that he will interpret and will choose to present in his own way. In this sense it is possible to interview someone in the same way that you write a novel or poetry.[4]

This conception of the interview as fiction describes the work method that he used with Velasco: "I interviewed him for many hours. He would tell me his story and I would listen to him like a psychoanalyst. I knew that there were gaps in his story from a literary point of view. Based on all the notes that I made, I then reconstructed his adventure. Not a single sentence in *The Story of a Shipwrecked Sailor* belongs to Velasco, but all the information comes from him. My task consisted of providing the literary framework for his story, of giving it the structure, touches and atmosphere that were necessary to interest the readers."[5] The first person narrative, as Gérard Genette points out, "lends itself better than any other to anticipation, by the very fact of its avowedly retrospective character, which authorizes the narrator to allude to the future and in particular to his present situation, for these to some extent form part of his role."[6] Since Velasco was still alive when the story appeared in *El Espectador*, the first person gave the text more authority and impact.

Raymond L. Williams affirms that "Velasco and his tale are fictionalized because the story is predominantly a creation of García Márquez the fiction writer, only disguised, at best, as García Márquez the journalist."[7] García Márquez the novelist produces a hybridized text by creating a double narrator, the Velasco-retrospective narrator and the Velasco-character narrator, who participated in the adventure. García Márquez reduces the distance between the two narrators to reactivate the immediacy of the event, as if it were occurring for the first time. This narrative strategy relates to the author's subversive intentions and clarifies his apparently contradictory dualist attitude about power: his imperious need to be at the center of power and close to those who hold it by whatever means, and his constant effort to undermine it through narrative discourse. For this reason, we can call García Márquez an "emergency politician."

His confrontation with the official world in *The Story of a Shipwrecked Sailor*, unlike the oblique encounters in the preceding series, drew an immediate response from High Command of the Navy on the republication of the story as a special supplement which included a number of compromising photographs. The letter which the High Command sent to *El Espectador* attempts to authenticate the official version: "The news stories and commentaries of *El Espectador* on the recent accident have failed to report accurately the facts of the case, and not only have they misinformed the public about the standard naval procedures concerning the handling of its ships and equipment, but they have also damaged the honor of the Navy and its members."[8] When García Márquez states in his preface to the 1970 edition that it is the first time that his name is linked with this text, he is not telling the whole truth. As Jacques Gilard points out, "he had already investigated the story of the sailor, and it is also revealing that in the space of several days he wrote three short articles about the case."[9]

After the publication of the special supplement, the two diametrically opposed positions on the accident crystallized. It seems plausible that from the outset García Márquez sensed the eventual outcome of the affair, and that, at each step, he consciously forced the authorities into a position which would put him on a collision course with the power structure to be able to oppose it from the inside. The systematic and exhaustive search for the accusatory photographs seems to confirm this dual position: "It was a direct confrontation of *El Espectador* with the power structure, and the already well-known reporter was becoming an outspoken critic of the dictatorship, capable of getting to the bottom of things which should be left unsaid."[10]

His accusation resides in the double narrator and, in addition, his retrospective narrator shows himself to be unreliable concerning the explanations, judgments and comments that the reader expects him to give. The double narrator counteracts the ostensible historical polyphony of the official version which presents several witnesses, all of whom focalize the event from the same perspective. In *The Story of a Shipwrecked Sailor*, several narrators present different points of view which create a dialogic polyphony. The author does not contest the fact that the accident took place; rather he torpedoes the official version in *how it occurred*.

The author obliquely incorporates the photographs of the illicit cargo into the story's most dramatic moment when Velasco is swept overboard. Once in the water, the character-narrator, through whose perspective the incident is primarily focalized, progressively reduces his field of vision until he focuses on the contraband cargo. He first realizes that he is completely alone, then he sees the destroyer in the distance. The range of his visual field decreases until he centers on the bobbing crates. His remark that he "had no idea what was happening" (18) reveals the presence of the retrospective narrator who refuses to intervene and explain his feelings. In this way the reader does not feel removed from the dramatic moment which retains its impact. Finally, the character-narrator's field of vision expands and he begins to contemplate the open sea.

Pedro Sorela states that "this tangential way of presenting the facts, although very effective in literary terms, undoubtedly relates closely to the caution exercised by the journalist in a repressive situation, and with the intention of outwitting the censors, who would have not permitted an open denunciation in the headlines and opening paragraphs of the story."[11] Sorela's explanation fails to elucidate the subversive act that this denunciation represents, given the particular framework in which it is made. The apparently "tangential way of presenting the facts" becomes a much stronger indictment, considering the reduction of Velasco's field of vision during the first moments in the water. We must also take into account the previous references to the contraband cargo to understand the full impact of the accusation in its human context.

In the first chapter, Velasco alludes to the contraband cargo when he describes his friend, Miguel Ortega, who used all his money to buy presents for his wife. Ortega had purchased "a refrigerator, an automatic washer, a radio, and a stove for them" (7). A little further on, Velasco refers to the delusive sense of security that the illicit cargo offers: "Amid the refrigerators, washing machines, and stoves that were tightly secured on the stern deck, Ramón Herrera and I lay down, carefully positioning ourselves to avoid being swept away by a wave" (14).

The author continues to contextualize the discourse until it appears for a third time in the most suspenseful and emotional moment of the story. He deliberately chooses this moment because it crystallizes the confrontation between his strong desire to approach the center of power and to undermine it through narrative discourse. He does not avoid the direct confrontation with censorship but endeavors to challenge it in a dialogic manner. The author recognizes that very utterance is situated in a context in which the centripetal and centrifugal forces clash continuously without any definite resolution. Every concrete utterance is characterized by hybridization and refraction. Hybridization involves two or more linguistic consciences within a single utterance which are frequently widely separated in time and social space. In a literary context, these hybrids are thus double-voiced and do not lead to any resolution.[12]   Refraction refers to the effect on authorial discourse as it passes through various other voices, and the word undergoes a "spectral dispersion." The word is directed at both an object and a receiver and its two paths "are strewn with previous claims that slow up, distort, refract the intention of the word."[13]   García Márquez produces a hybrid text and refracts the military discourse which passes through various discursive and human zones until it reappears in the dramatic moment of the story.

The letter sent to *El Espectador* from the information officer of the Navy contains not the start of this process but rather the flash point in the trajectory of the military discourse. The letter accuses the newspaper's management of "treating in a flippant and undignified manner a tragedy which can occur wherever naval vessels are operating; and despite the mourning and suffering that strike seven respectable Colombian families and all the members of the Navy, the newspaper saw no difficulty in publishing articles by rank amateur reporters who lack any knowledge about the subject, articles full of erroneous and technically inaccurate information, put in the mouth of the fortunate and worthy sailor who courageously saved his own life."[14] This passage tries to close the gaps that the story opens in the military discourse by addressing the mass of words which do not reside in the object (the accident) but in the collective conscience of the readers (the receiver).   The letter strains to monologize language, impose and unify the linguistic reality which surrounds the accident.   Quite the contrary, the words like "mourning," "suffering," "can occur wherever naval vessels are operating" and "full of erroneous and technically inaccurate information," reveal the apprehension of the military hierarchy, accustomed to vertical command, which now faces the possibility of seeing its official account subverted by the publication of the special supplement. The dictatorship of Rojas Pinilla, like all dictatorships, depends on monological language to guarantee, justify and prolong its existence, and it constantly exposes its own fragility to the inherently dialogical nature of the world.

This same discourse, once published and disseminated through various communication channels, can be subjected to the centrifugal forces of dialogic interaction (the same dictatorship closed several newspapers, and *El Espectador* had to suspend publication in December, 1955 due to maneuvers by the government). García Márquez seems to have recognized the vulnerability of the military discourse long before he undertook his subversive act. He contributed to channeling the military discourse through certain discursive zones which would distort and modify it until gaps and fissures opened in its monoglottic solidity.

The military discourse undergoes a series of modifications between its monologic form in the letter from the Navy's information officer and its altered representation in the story. The author starts by detaching the military discourse from its official context to be able to locate it in the human context in which the contraband cargo acquires a different meaning. In the first passage in the story, the cargo appears in an innocent light since chief gunner's mate Miguel Ortega invested all his money in gifts for his wife, including a refrigerator, an automatic washer, a radio and a stove. The words are refracted because they follow two different paths which lead simultaneously to an object (the contraband cargo) and to a receiver (the sailors). The mere presence of the cargo calls into question the military authority to which this discourse is addressed because, apparently, the same sailors do not realize that the navy is committing an illegal act. The double narrator guarantees the revitalization of the event as a lived experience. The author continues to subject the object (the illicit cargo to which the letter does not refer) to the centrifugal forces constituted by the purely personal motives of the sailors for buying this merchandise. The author again addresses the mass of external words in the collective conscience of the readers so that they themselves can modify and refract the military discourse. The personal framing of the cargo creates a series of norms which counterbalance the military norms of patriotism, danger, mourning, sacrifice, tragedy and national honor set forth in the letter. These same objects will later contribute to the death of seven of the eight sailors, and the author wants to expose this aspect of the merchandise.

In the second passage, the author establishes another norm which also opposes the military norms: the idea of security. The cargo is subjected to the centrifugal force of the sailors' discourse that expresses complete confidence in the chain of command (they believe that the cargo is tightly secured on the stern deck), in a system that requires its members to accept its discourse without question. The author adds several meteorological details which exclude the possibility of a storm as the cause of the accident: "There was no storm; the day was perfectly clear, visibility total, and the sky a deep blue" (15). By including the same objects in each part, the author progressively constructs a Gestalt image. The different perspectives concerning the contraband cargo enable the reader to form a more complete image by supplying what is missing, that is, those details which the Navy High Command deleted for understandable reasons. The author emphasizes the complete lack of awareness of the sailors regarding the illegality of the cargo, and this is one of the main points that he wants to underscore without stating it. He thus converts the objects into self-accusation by unleashing the conflictive discourses that surround the objects and which follow a path leading directly to the military establishment.

The contraband cargo furnishes the sailors with a transitory and deceptive feeling of happiness and security. In the third passage, the author places the objects at the center of the tragedy and their dispersion in the water undermines all the previous norms. Velasco stays afloat amid this objectal flotsam which denounces and deconstructs the military authority. García Márquez affirms in the preface of the 1970 edition that "the truth, never published until then, was that the ship, tossed violently by the wind in heavy seas, had spilled its ill-secured cargo and the eight sailors overboard" (viii). He adds that "the account, like the destroyer, was loaded with an ill-secured moral and political cargo that we hadn't foreseen" (viii). Considering the present analysis, García Márquez was most likely already aware of the "moral and political cargo" that the story contained. His double link with power helps establish a well-defined trajectory for his confrontation with the dictatorship which he puts on a collision course with the discursive conflict swirling around the contraband cargo.

If, as Pedro Sorela says, the censorship "would not have permitted an open denunciation in the headlines and opening paragraphs of the story," this is one more reason for García Márquez to rely on narrative discourse to subvert the military discourse. If the theme of power has been a constant in his work, and if, as he says, "absolute power is the highest and most complex of human achievements," it seems perfectly logical to find his subversion of power coupled with a fascination and a certain obsession with the same phenomenon. The same García Márquez witnesses and observes the exercise of power as if it were a feature film, and he the only viewer. Like the film viewer who remains separated from the screen and whose indirect involvement in the film creates a peculiar psychological relationship, that of García Márquez with power leads to the twin phenomenon of spectacularization and specularization.

Violette Morin distinguishes a tripartite division of spectacularization concerning the journalistic treatment of information:

> An event which a person reads about contains, in the *contemporary* press, a more or less considerable spectacular value in accordance with certain ways of presenting it. Reading about an event "as if you were there" means being absorbed by a more or less *live* spectacle, that is, more or less *seen and lived*. Next comes the *photograph*. The photograph, an ideal method of communication, supplies, whatever its technical and trick methods, an objective vision of the event; it overcomes the neutrality or increases the pleasure of each reader in its back and forth relationship with the written text. The third degree of spectacularization, *the written word*, makes the reader

pass from the *seen* to the *lived*, from the pictorial mode of expression to active mode, that is, the verbs. Verbs more or less revitalize the event, they seek to synchronize the moment in which the event has taken place with the moment in which the newspaper is being read.[15]

García Márquez restores the human dimension of the event so that the reader can witness the unfolding drama of Velasco as if it were taking place for the first time. The author merges the *seen* and the *lived* to create what is called in electronic journalism "live coverage" in which the words of the reporter are broadcast without being scripted. Moreover, the narrative follows the action so closely that they can almost be considered as simultaneous. The double narrator enables the author to achieve the same effect. The creation of a Gestalt image through the clash of discourses and languages surrounding the contraband cargo crystallizes the historical event in the reader's mind, and he proceeds to furnish the missing details.

The author succeeds in transforming the accusatory photos into narrative discourse by constantly stressing the presence of the objects. He also reactivates the different discourses that the official world tried in vain to silence. Beyond the visual impact of the photographs, their reassimilation into the narrative reveals the subversive strategy of the author. He not only succeeds in spectacularizing the story's most dramatic moment on the textual level by employing action and visual verbs, but he also skillfully synchronizes the two moments mentioned by Violette Morin to create live coverage which is *seen* and *lived*.

The Story of a Shipwrecked Sailor confirms the corrosive power of narrative and shows the dualist position of García Márquez before the phenomenon of power: an attraction-repulsion movement which impels the author to find the power center and subvert it without losing its specular value. Specularization constitutes a fundamental aspect in the bigeneric writing of García Márquez. Drawing close to power does not signify being absorbed, nor much less corrupted, by this phenomenon, but it signals a profound desire to observe it from the absolute center. The subversion of power through narrative discourse cannot bring about a final defeat because, in the dialogic world in which the author is writing and living, there exists no first nor final word. The discourse of power, whether dictatorial or revolutionary, constitutes one of the numerous discourses populating the dialogical world. The author combats it most effectively by activating and setting in motion other discourses which oppose it. García Márquez knows very well that for the writer, faced with the forces of oppression, narrative discourse offers him the best weapon in this struggle. Nevertheless, despite all the efforts to define the political stance of García Márquez, there remains his specular fascination with power. This obsession manifests itself in his different narrative strategies which allow him to occupy a position similar to that advocated by Gustave Flaubert: the author resembles God, invisible but omnipresent. This characterization of the author's posture with respect to his work epitomizes the dualist attitude of García Márquez regarding the enthralling theme of power.

Notes

1.   The adventure story of the sailor Luis Alejandro Velasco appeared in *El Espectador* on April 5, 6, 9, 11, 12, 13, 14, 15, 16, 18, 19, 20, 21, and 22, 1955 and carried the title "The Truth About My Adventure." In addition, a special supplement was published on April 28 with the title "The Odyssey of the Survivor of the *ARC Caldas*. The Truth About My Adventure." Jacques Gilard explains that "in the brief presentation of the fourteen part series, it is pointed out that it was GGM who wrote the complete text; in this special supplement various photographs are included, in particular those which establish beyond a shadow of a doubt that the ship was loaded with contraband cargo." Gabriel García Márquez, *Obra periodística Vol. 2: Entre cachacos I*, ed. Jacques Gilard (Barcelona: Bruguera, 1982), 98. Ensuing quotes appear in the text with page numbers in parentheses. Translations are mine.

2.   Gabriel García Márquez and Plinio Apuleyo Mendoza, *The Fragrance of Guava*, trans. Ann Wright (London: Verso, 1983), 88.

3.   Gabriel García Márquez, *The Story of a Shipwrecked Sailor*, trans. Randolph Hogan (New York: Vintage Books, 1987), vii. All ensuing quotes appear in the text with page numbers in parentheses.

4.   Pierre Boncenne, "Gabriel García Márquez s'explique," *Lire* 51 (November, 1979), 55. Translations are mine.

5.   Pierre Boncenne, "Gabriel García Márquez s'explique," 57.

6.   Gérard Genette, *Narrative Discourse: An Essay in Method*, trans. Jane E. Lewin (Ithaca: Cornell UP, 1983), 67.

7.   Raymond L. Williams, *Gabriel García Márquez* (Boston: Twayne, 1984), 28.

8.   *Entre cachacos I*, 78.

9.   *Entre cachacos I*, 76.

10.   *Entre cachacos I*, 79.

11.   Pedro Sorela, *El otro García Márquez: Los años difíciles* (Madrid: Mondadori, 1988), 153. Translation is mine.

12.   See footnote 40, Chapter 3, page 87.

13.   M. M. Bakhtin, *The Dialogic Imagination: Four Essays*, trans. Caryl Emerson and Michael Holquist (Austin: University of Texas Press, 1981), 432.

14.   *Entre cachacos I*, 65.

15.   Violette Morin, *El tratamiento periodístico de la información*, trans. Alfonso Espinet (Barcelona: Mouton and Co. and ATE, 1974), 35-6. Translation is mine.

Chapter 6

The Politics of Narration or How to Narrate Politics: García Márquez's Series on La Sierpe

Introduction: A Change of Heart

In 1952, the first installment of García Márquez's series on the Atlantic Coast region called La Sierpe appeared in the short-lived magazine *Lámpara*, a publication of the International Petroleum Company (ESSO).[1] *El Espectador* published the rest of the chronicle in its "Sunday Magazine" section in March and April, 1954. According to Jacques Gilard, García Márquez had obtained his information "in the 40s through numerous conversations held in Sucre, where many stories were circulating about that strange region, although he singles out Angel Casi Palencia as his principal source, a friend who lived in Sucre and then Cartagena."[2] The series attests to García Márquez's sustained interest in his native costeño culture, and his approach emphasizes the centrality of the human context. His intention is not to analyze the customs, religious and social practices, for this perspective would silence the voices emanating from this culture, and would impose a single viewpoint on the multifaceted composition of costeño culture. His approach replaces monologue with dialogue in which many voices participate, and the customs, beliefs and superstitions are continuously revitalized by the heterophony of alterity.

García Márquez's narrative strategy in this series is determined in part by the nature of the material. He is dealing with a collective phenomenon whose events he has collected from his informant and other anonymous sources. His task involves both journalistic and literary considerations which lead to an interplay between narrator and information sources. Not only does García Márquez refuse to silence these anonymous sources, but he incorporates them into his dialogic narrative form.

García Márquez also faced the problem of naturalizing the peculiar reality of this material for his readers. As the introduction

175

to the *Lámpara* article indicates, the reality depicted by Gabriel García Márquez belongs to magical realism: "La Sierpe, a labyrinth of thick undergrowth and bogs, a kingdom of enchantments, sorcery and evil spells, is neither a mythic region, nor a poisonous aspic, but a coastal region steeped in Spanish love, African superstitions and impenetrable mystery."[3] This description also situates the text in the "real world" by giving it a geographical designation (coastal region). The author further establishes the "objective" reality of this region by noting that a certain Doctor Manuel Zapata Olivella "brought a musical group from that region which surprises even the best informed people" (867). These superficial observations confirm that there is "still a lot to be discovered in the national spirit," and that these articles will reveal "the multiple manifestations of a very singular life style which could fill a whole volume on the history of Colombian folklore" (867). García Márquez's ostensible role consists of giving readers "entertaining descriptions of such a rich and relatively unknown topic" (867). This introduction addresses itself to incredulous readers who will rely on the authority of the "costeño intellectual" for these entertaining descriptions. While these articles contribute to the "dissemination of Colombian culture and Colombianism" (867), the introduction clearly distinguishes between fact and fiction. The introduction in *Lámpara* places García Márquez in the position of a narrator-critic whose primary function is to describe La Sierpe without resorting to the sources of information. "Entertaining descriptions" voice over the human polyphony which infuses the reality of La Sierpe.

The series undergoes some changes between 1952 and its republication in 1954. The *Lámpara* article's title "La Sierpe" expands to "La Marquesita of La Sierpe" when it appears in *El Espectador*. García Márquez adds subheadings in the second version which reflect a journalistic practice of capturing the reader's attention and furnishing them with a kernel or microversion of the content. The subheading in *Lámpara*, "A Region on the Atlantic Coast," also expands in the second version: "Malaria, Sorcery and Superstitions in a Region of the Atlantic Coast. The Man Who Stumbled Upon the Legend." The inclusion of La

Marquesita in the second title signals a shift in García Márquez's attitude toward the articles. La Marquesita will produce intertextual resonances in García Márquez's fiction, most notably in Big Mama ("Big Mama's Funeral"), Ursula (*OHYS*) and Bendición Alvarado (*AP*). In the La Sierpe series, besides occupying the top rung of the social ladder, La Marquesita possesses the most important powers. A second change occurs in the subsection where García Márquez substitutes the word "region" for "country." However slight the modification, it points to the technique of imprecise precision which García Márquez uses in dealing with geography.[4] The word "region" connotes more ill-defined geographical parameters than the word "country."

The geographical location of La Sierpe is also slightly modified. In the *Lámpara* article, "La Sierpe is not a prison. It is much easier to get there than to Leticia, Ocaña or any other of the towns located in Quindio. Nor is it unusual to talk about it" (868). The new version removes geographical markers: "It is nothing new to talk about La Sierpe, since the rice dealers..."[5] Again, geographic imprecision takes precedence over locating La Sierpe in relation to other places. As the expanded subheading of the second version indicates, García Márquez emphasizes La Sierpe's remoteness: "One Way Trip." The deletion of the first part of the paragraph in the subsequent article removes the mental map which offers the readers a convenient way of situating La Sierpe. The three words of the second subheading---malaria, sorcery and superstitions---suggest a negative, albeit mysterious, mixture which will subsequently be turned into positive qualities: "Nothing will make the inhabitants of the Sierpe leave their inferno of malaria, sorcery, animals and superstitions" (118). Finally, the last phrase of the expanded subheading, "The Man Who Stumbled Upon the Legend," counterbalances the first part by introducing the cultural code of folklore and legend.

Increasing the Possibilities: From Phenotext to Genotext

The opening sentences of the revised version perform several functions: "Several years ago a ghostly, glassy-looking man, with a big stomach as taut as a drum, came to a doctor's office in the city. He said: 'Doctor, I have come to have you remove a monkey that was put in my belly'" (117). The text opens *in media res* with an event which is then suspended. García Márquez frequently resorts to this technique in his journalism and fiction.[6]   This beginning captures the reader's attention and immediately introduces a series of sociocultural oppositions/mirrors: patient-farmer/doctor-city, city/La Sierpe, medicine-science/medicine-folklore, science/sorcery and objective/marvelous reality. While the campesino's words are given in tagged direct discourse and indicate a strong narrative presence, the sentence itself negates zero focalization. The sentence is, using J.L. Austin's terms, both locutionary (forming a sentence) and illocutionary (the production of the sentence constitutes in itself a certain act).[7]   The illocutionary aspect of his sentence represents a strong request (to have you remove a monkey), but the perlocutionary function of the sentence (the act of enunciation serves more distant ends) is not carried out.[8] In this case, perlocution means persuading the doctor to cure him. The sentence remains constative (it tends only to describe an event) and not performative (the expression describes a certain action accomplished by its speaker and producing this expression amounts to accomplishing that action).[9]

Although the event is displaced and the dialogue fails to fulfill its perlocutionary function and thereby indicates a selective absence (or use) of zero focalization, the author uses this temporally suspended event to introduce one of the other narrative voices. This first breach of zero focalization opens the way for creating an opposition within the text "insofar as the text is a writing on a dual basis that opens the 'inside' of the sign to the 'outside' of significance."[10] The opposition arises between the phenotext "where the signifying activity is phenomenalized, spread out flat in a structured signification" and the genotext "which is made up of the signifiers in their infinite differentiation."[11]

In the first chronicle, the phenotext constitutes the written text whose signifying activity is controlled by the nonfocalized narrator. The genotext can be identified as the oral text which will be engendered by breaches in the zero focalization, so that "a reader can receive a written message orally and an oral message in written form."[12] As these gaps in focalization multiply, two levels of discourse---narrative and cultural---and two levels of reality---objective and marvelous---alternate within the boundaries of the text as the author increasingly exposes zero focalization to the polyphonic presence of other narrative voices. In this way, the phenotextual signs open up to the genotextual signifiers in their infinite differentiation. The following diagram shows how these two levels function in the first chronicle:

I.   Phenotext -- single nonfocalized narrator -- objective reality -- narrative discourse (story) -- univocal sign system

II.   Genotext -- polyphonic narrators -- marvelous reality -- cultural discourse -- polyvalent sign system

The chronicle opens with the man coming to the doctor's office so that he can remove "a monkey that they put in my belly" (117). This story component is then transferred to "La Sierpe, a legendary region," or to a different plane of reality. In La Sierpe, the surprising request made by the man at the outset becomes "one of the most common occurrences of daily life" (117). The strange becomes the commonplace in this domain of magical reality, and a curse can be placed on an offender whereby "a monkey is born, grows and reproduces in his stomach" (117). The reality of this curse is marked by the use of gradation (born, grows, reproduces). The sign becomes permutable and identifies itself with a whole group of beliefs (curses, supernatural powers, superstitions) which underpin the society of La Sierpe.

In the first paragraph, zero focalization quickly gives way to internal focalization, and direct tagged discourse changes to indirect discourse marked by the verb "he explained" (117). The chronicle rapidly moves to the second level as the character-narrator establishes the geographic remoteness of La Sierpe through imprecise precision and the repetition of the word "beyond." As Wilfrido H. Corral states, García Márquez "sets up a fusion of the chronicle and short story codes and establishes a metanarrative interplay between the narrator and the sources of information which leads the reader to discard an extratextual referent."[13]   La Sierpe's geographical inaccessibility paves the way for its insertion into the marvelous reality daily where occurrences are considered fantastic in objective terms. In other words, the narrative movement is one of mirrors-mirages as elements (the monkey in the man's stomach) pass from one reality to another.

The reader learns that La Sierpe is a common topic of conversation and that the rice dealers of San Jorge know that a high quality rice grows there. This rice can be purchased at normal prices "in spite of transportation problems" (117). Since the reader's frame of reference is now marvelous reality, he is able to reach La Sierpe. After a journey by boat, pack animal and a two-day trip through the swamps, "the traveler will reach the swamps of La Sierpe" (118). Another geographical twist is introduced because "the difficult part is the return trip" (118). Finally, the traveler who ventures into this "swampy, overgrown region where only a few rays of sunshine can be seen in widely scattered spots" will find people "who don't look any racially different from ordinary Colombians" (118). In La Sierpe "there are good and bad people, like everywhere, [who] enjoy themselves like everybody else" (118). These references assimilating the inhabitants of La Sierpe to a common cultural denominator conceal more than they reveal, because they refer to extratextual norms which are difficult to verify by objective means. These same references, however, naturalize the text for the reader and prepare him to enter this society which lives according to a different reality. According to Jonathan Culler, naturalization "emphasizes the fact that the strange or deviant is brought within a discursive order and thus made to seem natural."[14]   The identification of the reader with a specific social group constitutes a way "of naturalizing the text and giving it a place in the world which our culture defines."[15]

The Reign of La Marquesita: Power and Its Narration

These signs deploy themselves along the flat plane of the phenotext and facilitate the insertion of two key elements which distinguish La Sierpe from other social groups: its religious practices and La Marquesita. Following a series of general cultural links, the author declares: "Nothing will make the inhabitants of La Sierpe leave their inferno of malaria, sorcery, animals and superstitions" (118). The inhabitants practice their religion "like the majority of Colombian campesinos" (118). They also "fall in love like Catholics and Spaniards" and "have Catholic marriages" (118). The genotext then displaces the phenotext and the reader passes from objective to marvelous reality through a kind of narrative slippage when he learns that "these people believe in God, in the Virgin and in the mystery of the Holy Trinity, but they worship them in any object in which they think they find divine powers, and they say prayers to them that they themselves have composed. But above all---and this is where they differ from the rest of the Colombians---they believe in La Marquesita" (119. This sentence transfers the reader to another level of reality and verisimilitude and prepares the way for what will follow in the rest of this chronicle and the other three.

The gaps created in the phenotext coincide with the breaches in zero focalization: "The oldest inhabitants of La Sierpe heard their grandparents say that many years ago a kind and diminutive Spanish woman lived in the region who possessed a fabulous fortune of animals, gold objects, precious stones, and who was known by the name of La Marquesita" (119). The author quickly abandons his role as the intellectual who will entertain his readers with a series of cultural oddities and anecdotes. In order to reach the significational diversity of the genotext, the author opens the narrative to other voices which resonate throughout the whole series. The visible but transitory presence of these other voices creates double-voiced discourse which "is characterized by the fact that not only is it represented but it also refers simultaneously to two contexts of enunciation: that of the present enunciation and that of a previous one."[16] The other's discourse can be present in varying degrees, ranging from explicit dialogue to an implicit presence. The voices in the La Sierpe series belong to this third degree of presence in which "the other's discourse receives no material corroboration and yet is summoned forth: it is because it is held available in the collective memory of a given social group."[17]

The brief duration of these anonymous voices can be partially explained by the fact that they constitute vestiges of a past which has always been dominated by a nonfocalized voice imposed from outside. From the time of the Conquest, this monoglottic voice has always co-opted and subjugated the native ones so that down through the centuries Latin American history has been a monochromatic record filtered through the eyes of different foreign powers. Only at the very beginning of the Conquest, before Western man started in earnest to imprint his vision on the continent, do we find the chronicles where history is infused with marvelous, magical qualities.

García Márquez often refers to these initial documents recording Western man's brief stay in Paradise. However, as Virgilio López Lemus explains, García Márquez is far from being a dreamy-eyed utopian:

> Nevertheless, García Márquez has not been the narrator of the new material life, of a new world social order which he has commented about in Latin America in reference to the socialist system in Cuba. The Colombian author works artistically with reality, that one which, according to him, does not end with the price of tomatoes, and the reality that he creates is very bitter, it is Latin American underdevelopment. The road leading to revolutionary transformation is also not expressed in his work, except in the symbolic examples that we have shown. He certainly is not yet singing the praises of the new order, nor is his work the literature of socialism, because the world which can be studied in his work is precisely that which requires socialism in order to come into being.[18]

For García Márquez, reality may not end with the price of tomatoes, but it is certainly an important factor in opting for one system over another.

García Márquez's choice of a narrative stance is also crucial because he realizes that if he were to devote himself entirely to social realism, he would run the same risk of imposing another form of sociocultural and narrative hegemony on his world. For García Márquez utopia lies neither in the remote past nor in the distant future, but within man himself in the present.[19] In *OHYS*, Melquíades, submerged in the predictions of Nostradamus, "thought he had found a prediction of the future of Macondo. It was to be a luminous city with great glass houses where there was no trace remaining of the race of the Buendías."[20] This vision points to a utopian impulse in García Márquez, but he knows that utopias have a way of evaporating in the harsh light of reality. Cuba's own attempt at socialism has run into serious obstacles, especially since 1970 when Castro tried to produce enough sugar to pay off its debt to the Soviet Union and steer an independent course. As attractive as Cuba may be to García Márquez, he knows that any literature indicating the way towards revolutionary transformation must be backed by the hard currency of reality before writers can give it artistic expression. The same criteria apply to the relative absence of African and Indian cultures in his works. In *OHYS*, the two Indians, Cataure and Visitación, leave little trace of their presence in the novel. The history of Pre-Columbian Indian cultures is a yawning gap which is impossible to reconstruct except through silent relics and secondhand sources. Most written records of these cultures constitute monological, univocal versions which suppress the native voices.

La Marquesita, as Wilfrido H. Corral says, "does not fit into any easily identifiable sociocultural category and with the addition of fantastic elements the referential dissolution underscores the genitive function of the character."[21] La Marquesita, who occupies the highest position in La Sierpe's social structure and who possesses the most marvelous powers (except the secret of eternal life which denies her immortality and opens the way to the other chronicles and especially to the figure of Jesusito who is her mirror image in a sense), acts as a nuclear core which generates the world of La Sierpe. Her physical appearance, life and secret powers reveal themselves in a series of metanarrative voices emanating from the legendary past: "According to the traditional story, the Spanish woman had white skin and blond hair, and never had a husband;" "Legend has it that La Marquesita lived for as long as she willed"; La Marquesita had a pact with the devil, as they explain in the Sierpe" (119-20). All knowledge about La Marquesita derives from popular and legendary sources, so that the reader has the impression that he is hearing/reading an oral/written message. The authority of the nonfocalized narrator is weakened by this constant interplay of oral/written texts which combine to create a collage portrait of La Marquesita.

Her physical traits suggest that she is a descendant of that small Spanish ruling class which did not intermarry (Spanish, white skin and blond hair), but no other details are given about her family past. Indeed, she seems to contradict the usual stereotype of the protected woman living in a male dominated society. Her powers and prestige belong to her alone, and no male has entered her life: "The Marquesita was a kind of Big Mama to those who served her in La Sierpe" (119). La Marquesita contradicts the traditional image of the woman within the socioeconomic structure of Latin American society, and she also reflects the strong matriarchal presence in Caribbean culture. Nothing about her is traditional, and she may also represent an ideological stance on García Márquez's part. Like other feminine figures in his fiction, most notably Big Mama and Ursula Iguarán, La Marquesita not only proves equal to men but overshadows them in every way: she has never had a husband or given birth to any offspring, and the source of her power is never revealed. These traits make her an independent woman who is subject and not object. This capacity to act as a subject could suggest García Márquez's own view of women within a different socioeconomic order, albeit socialist.

Power, whether human or natural, and however absolute, cannot exceed certain limits, and La Marquesita is not exempted:

"The only thing she couldn't do was to bring the dead back to life because the souls of the dead didn't belong to her" (119). Her long life, like those of dictators who believe they are immortal, comes to an end, and the ultimate power is denied her: "Before dying, La Marquesita passed on many of her secrets to her faithful followers, except the secret of eternal life" (120). Although it is difficult to envisage the story of La Marquesita as a political parable, it is clear that the image of this matriarch, like much of the reality surrounding dictators (García Márquez encountered the same phenomenon in Stalin when he visited the Soviet Union in 1957), emanates from the multitude of popular-turned-legendary oral sources to which García Márquez gives expression. La Marquesita's death moves heaven and earth: "Her death was preceded by heavenly signs, telluric upheavals and the bad dreams of the inhabitants of La Sierpe" (120). Like many dictators, La Marquesita leaves behind a legendary aura and the inhabitants of La Sierpe believe that La Marquesita's treasure and the secret of eternal life are buried in the middle of the swamp which she created as her final act.

The first chronicle concludes with a story that demonstrates how discourse deriving from popular and traditional sources augments the stature of La Marquesita. The nonfocalized narrator transfers his narrative functions to "a well-known person in the surrounding villages of La Sierpe," or "street voice" in Vargas Llosa's term ("The same person tells...." "...Legend has it that...."), and finally, he distances himself even further from the story: "The description the man gives of his adventure is as fantastic as the legend of La Marquesita" (121). This statement amounts to a paralipsis "by means of which one declares that one is not saying what one is saying in the sentence itself."[22] In other words, the adventure recounted by the man is just as credible-incredible or real-unreal as La Marquesita's story, and reality can take many forms, albeit fantastic. Like many quest stories, it is not the attainment of the goal but the quest which is the most crucial, and this man "is the person who has come the closest to finding La Marquesita's treasures" (120). The final prize ultimately eludes the greedy adventurer, but he "retained the satisfaction of being the only man in La Sierpe to have dared to venture into the realm of legend" (121). This adventure story increases the legendary aura surrounding La Marquesita, a variant focalized through a character who temporarily displaces the nonfocalized narrator. Reality is transformed by its link to the marvelous real and by the absence of value judgments and commentaries by the nonfocalized narrator. The reality of this story is difficult to analyze in objective terms, and it completes the movement of the narrative from the daily to the marvelous plane of reality on which the society engendered by La Marquesita exists. The fact that her treasures are never found also leaves the way open for the creation of this society based on the hierarchization of power. Since no one possesses the secret of eternal life, power, whatever its nature and however extensive it may be, encounters the natural limitation of death.

In La Marquesita's Wake: La Sierpe and the Distribution of Power

In "The Supernatural Legacy of La Marquesita," the society to which the legacy of her powers gives rise, is a logical extension of her own life. Since she bequeathed her powers to her preferred followers, they are now divided among different people who enjoy the exclusive possession of one power. This "exclusive possession of the powers has given rise to a very well-defined social hierarchy whose top is composed of families who hold the secrets for clearing away things and whose bottom consists of families who possess the secrets to cure dog mange" (137). This society exists within the confines of magical reality: "Some of the extraordinary secret powers of the Marquesita were shared by her with those faithful who were closest to her and they have been passed down through time with the prestige of a birthright" (136).

In this society, power, although hierarchized, is controlled by various factors which constitute an effective system of checks and balances. In each family, the person who possesses a given power "can enjoy it, but an insignificant act of negligence by the owner, the slightest indiscretion that endangers the sole ownership of the power, suffices to negate its effectiveness" (136). One disobedient and spendthrift member lost the power of walking on water when he bet on it in a card game. Power in this society is self-regulating so that, despite its different degrees, no one can exceed certain boundaries without being punished. The structure of this society offers a certain parallel with García Márquez's socialist vision of the early Macondo in which everyone is considered "equal" in spite of real differences, and everyone shares in the community's life. The society of La Sierpe takes into account the real differences which exist in any power structure, but even those who do not possess supernatural powers are equal: "But the possibility of saving their souls ennobles those people because the possession and use of all forms of power necessarily imply 'a pact with the devil'" (137).

In the second chronicle, the narrator, drawing on the voices from the popular and legendary sources of an oral tradition which help complete the transition from objective to marvelous reality in the first chronicle, remains within this framework. The internal structure of this society does not require any detailed explanation since the narrator's stance harmonizes with the limitations imposed on him by his material. More important, the narrator's view of reality coincides with that La Sierpe so that its marginality is not emphasized. It is not surprising that García Márquez situates his fiction in socioculturally marginal and rural areas whose isolation is repeatedly disrupted by outside forces. García Márquez is not a utopian writer advocating a return to the past by shutting the door to all intruders, but invariably, exterior forces have two primary characteristics: they usually impose themselves on the community and their primary goal is some form of exploitation. These forces, whether political, social, economic or cultural, inevitably become marginalized in relation to the society they are invading: "The social marginality which characterizes the people of La Sierpe coincides with groups who live on the margin of the fundamentally rural society of the author and his work: gringos, Syrians, gypsies, Europeans. Obviously, the society is constructed with little outside influence, and its thought is sustained by the beliefs of its citizens."[23] La Sierpe's marginality serves to magnify the opposite form of marginality which usually accompanies the incursion of outside forces. In La Sierpe, however, we do not witness the procession of exterior forces which besiege Macondo.

La Sierpe constitutes a microcosm of a society which has decided to construct its socioeconomic structure according to a set of internal principles. For better or worse, this society has made a conscious choice to create its own socioeconomic system. In this society, the capitalist work ethic that one can get ahead without hurting one's neighbor does not play a role. In La Sierpe, the personal worth of one's work prevails. Alongside the families possessing the powers inherited from La Marquesita we find "the holder of the powers to cure snake bites" (137). Even though the curandero is a marginal member of this society, certain conditions have converted him into "a high priest, and the lives of his neighbors depend on his care and discretion" (137). The curandero does not accept money for his services "because it would render his power useless" (137). Buying his services means turning his power into an object to be bought and sold, a medium of exchange which is incompatible with this society. Instead, he agrees "to having the patient or his family work for him or give him gifts and animals" (137). The curandero is not interested in "getting ahead" or competing with his neighbors, and his work represents an integral expression of his person: "The possessor of the power against snake bites is thoroughly convinced of his abilities: he never hurries" (138).

While García Márquez is fully cognizant that absolute equality, both in terms of the social structure and the distribution of power within La Sierpe or any society, is not achievable in practical terms, the infrastructure of La Sierpe suggests that *relative* equality is an attainable goal. This relative equality emerges in the discussion of the most valuable power inherited from La Marquesita: the power to clear away. The possessor of this power "also enjoys the opposite power," so that he "can, if he wishes, cause his enemy's field to become densely overgrown and useless with the same powers" (138). Other powers inherited from La Marquesita (in descending order of importance) include the ability to cure cattle of worms, stop hemorrhaging, give birth without pain, locate a person from any distance and, finally, the secret of how a wife can hang on to her husband. This last power is the least prized because La Marquesita died a virgin and "it's believed that she never had any sexual problems and, therefore, the secret of holding on to the husband can't belong to her" (139). Other powers offset the low esteem in which this last one is held. They are based on "human experience, a knowledge of botany, and the properties of animal organs" (139) and are generally practiced by women. With them women can produce "temporary impotence in unfaithful husbands" or "make an enemy's stomach burst forth with a swarm of little animals in the intestines" (139-40). The internal system of checks and balances continuously regulates the distribution of power in La Sierpe.

The possession and use of a specific power, whatever its value and function within this society, do not guarantee domination and autonomy. Even the families who inherited the Marquesita's powers incur limitations: "The biblical exchange of the plate of lentils is impossible to repeat as are the secret powers of the elders of the Sierpe" (136). The "work" which the power holders perform is not a consumer good. The treatment of work as a consumer good results in the loss of the power, in a double form of social and economic alienation. When a person turns his power into a product, "the product ceases to be the objective embodiment of the individual's own personality and the distinctive expression of his creative powers and interests."[24] In La Sierpe, each member possesses one power which he exercises in a distinctive manner, and his "work" is a form of self-expression. The powers within La Sierpe are mostly preventive in nature, and they are not used to produce objects and goods for sale.

The work ethic in La Sierpe does not relate to the Puritan version which advocated sacrifice, hard work, frugality and shunned any outward display of wealth. Profits were reinvested in one's business, and this helped spawn the capitalist system. In La Sierpe the profit motive is absent: "The exercise of the powers inherited from La Marquesita is considered an honorable trade. Whoever has one power does not exercise the opposite power under normal circumstances, except to defend his life or that of his family or the possession of the same power" (139). In other words, competition is ruled out, and no one uses a given power to get ahead of someone else. No apparent difference exists between mental and physical work in the exercise of power, a division which accentuates and accelerates the process of alienation and the creation of a class system. All of the powers in La Sierpe are "useful to a marginal society that does not take on the outside functions of a developed capitalist country."[25] Besides representing much more than an example of Colombian folklore which García Márquez is trying to rescue from oblivion, La Sierpe offers the vision of a society which resembles Macondo during its early, autonomous stage when it still can choose to create its own history. The socioeconomic infrastructure of La Sierpe embodies several important principles---relative equality, a more even distribution of power and work as an expression of personal worth---which this society has created for itself.

Economics and Religion: Further Permutations of Power in La Sierpe

In "The Strange Idolatry of the Sierpe," the author shows how La Sierpe handles the problem of consumption of goods linked to religion. The event which gives rise to the worship of the idol, Jesusito, originates in a product of a consumer society. A woman carrying a wooden box filled with soap notices that a piece of it has come loose. After carefully examining the piece of wood, she "saw the image of the Virgin in the rough surface. The consecration was immediate and the canonization direct, without metaphors nor circumlocutions: Saint Plank" (145). Religion, economics and society combine to produce an event in which the values from the three areas coalesce. Saint Plank performs miracles (Catholic usage) and is passed around during prayer "when winter threatens the crops" (145) (a good example of how religious syncretism functions in "primitive" polytheistic societies). This initial event leads to "an extravagant and numerous collection of saints" (145) who serve many different functions in this society. This interfusion of Catholicism and a kind of polytheistic shamanism demonstrates how this society has established a bicultural dialogue with an outside force (Christianity) and has succeeded in integrating it into its belief system without serious disruptions in the fabric of society.

The inhabitants have adapted the practice of sanctifying to their own needs in order to create a gallery of saints like Saint Table, Saint Kidney and the most popular of all, Jesusito. Jesusito, like many Catholic relics and saints, has become a consumer product, but his economic value differs greatly from the way in which many religious objects in a capitalist system are mass-produced in such quantity that they turn into souvenirs whose meaning is lost. There is only one Jesusito and later on, when the idol is stolen, and many copies start to appear, the reaction of the inhabitants of La Sierpe is revealing. So many imitations appear that "eight months after being lost, the prestige of Jesusito began to be questioned. The faith of its followers wavered, and the pile of questionable idols was burned because somebody assured them that the real Jesusito was impervious to fire" (148). The relationship between object and owner (or producer) is one to one, and the mass production of Jesusitos not only threatens the faith of the followers, but also disrupts the personal bond between them. The introduction of a capitalist method (a large scale production of apocryphal Jesusitos) runs counter to the fundamental values of this society.

Jesusito is the counter-mirror image of La Marquesita: "Jesusito has not only replaced La Marquesita as the social axis, but the concept of the axis of the social pyramid has also passed from user to used."[26] Even though Jesusito is a consumer product which circulates among the inhabitants of La Sierpe and has different "owners," his authenticity remains inviolable: "It is a niche composed of royal palm leaves, in whose center, on a small box lined with brightly colored paper, there sits the most popular and most visited idol in the region: a little black man, two inches high, carved out of a piece of wood and mounted on a gold ring. He has a simple and familiar name: Jesusito. And he is invoked by the inhabitants of La Sierpe in any emergency" (146). Not only is he invested with miraculous powers, but he is subject "to the law

of supply and demand. This coveted object, which can be obtained
through honest dealings, adequately compensates the buyers who
have made sacrifices" (146).   For La Sierpe's inhabitants, he is
not a product of a disposable consumer society but an object that
"has been passed down from generation to generation and has
been a means of support throughout the years to those who have
been its different owners" (146). Jesusito is not a "product" of La
Sierpe because he "is a venerable saint, of unknown origin" (146).
In this economic system, the object amasses riches and not its
owner: "Traditionally, Jesusito's owner also has the right to the
charitable and votive offerings of gold, but not to the animals
which are offered to the idol in order to increase its private
patrimony" (146). It is the possession and not the possessor of
Jesusito which can lead to the creation of a profitable business like
that of the cattle rancher who "sold off his cattle and land, and
started to wander through all the villages, going from festival to
festival with his prosperous shop of miracles" (146).   Mass
production is not valued in this society and "the productive
marginality of that system becomes evident when the consumption
of an idolatry arises whose axis is not in a position to change that
marginality."[27]

　　　Jesusito's disappearance causes the inhabitants to undertake
a frantic search which seems fantastic given the size of the idol:
"In order to find him, all the inhabitants of the region were busy for
three hundred sixty-five days and nights" (147). After the robber
threw Jesusito in the garden, "the faithful immediately started to
clear the garden, inch by inch" (147). When all their efforts fail to
turn up the idol, an expert in such matters proposes a fiesta as the
way to make him reappear. Just when all seems hopeless, the idol
suddenly reappears in the middle of the road some distance from
the garden. Jesusito is immediately thrown into a bonfire and
"when the fire died out, the idol was there, its authentic shape of
Jesusito perfectly intact" (149). This event marked "the start of
the private fortune of Jesusito [who] receives head of cattle and
good grazing land with running water from his worshippers" (149).

Jesusito's owner acts as the administrator of his wealth. Jesusito's wealth reflects the social values of this primarily agrarian society, and precious metals, such as gold and silver, do not constitute coveted objects. Jesusito's disappearance also caused a serious disruption in the agricultural economy of La Sierpe: "It was a bad year for La Sierpe. The harvests declined, the quality of the seeds decreased and earning weren't high enough to take care of the region's basic needs, which were never so pressing as in that year" (148). Neither La Marquesita nor Jesusito exceeds the value boundaries of this society which has exercised, on however small a scale, its right to make internal choices concerning the socioreligious and economic structure which best fits its needs. Its marginality serves as a mirror in which other forms of marginality become intensified (both internal and external forces). La Sierpe has been able to integrate and adapt the person of the La Marquesita and the object of Jesusito to its internal needs within a rather loosely organized and fluid social structure.

These texts present a problem of verisimilitude since it is difficult to distinguish between levels of discourse (historical, political and economic) and what might be termed "short story discourse." Even García Márquez's political articles most often take the form of a story. These chronicles also appear as a series of loosely connected stories, and that may explain why Jesusito suddenly disappears as the central focus and is replaced by a fundamental concern of society: death. Death involves an activity central to La Sierpe---the wake---which supplants Jesusito as the socioeconomic and religious focal point: "Housewives in La Sierpe go shopping every time a person dies. The wake is the centerpiece of a social and commercial activity in a region whose inhabitants do not have any other opportunity to get together and enjoy themselves except when the death of someone they know brings them together" (150). The internal values of this isolated society produce other forms of marginalization which, in this case, is the dead person who should be the center of attention. On the contrary, once he is put in "the most obscure corner where the deceased will not be an obstacle, where he will be the least trouble," then people "go straight to the patio of the house and set up stands along the fence where they sell knick-knacks, fried foods, cheap lotions and matches. When night comes, the patio is transformed into a public market" (150). The deceased serves as a catalyst for economic and social activities.

La Marquesita as a representative of a society based on hereditary power, Jesusito as a coveted object of high monetary value and the dead person, undergo transformations which contradict the values of a bourgeois society. While the power of the Marquesita is dispersed and distributed throughout the society, Jesusito and the dead man set in motion the economic and social machinery. In La Sierpe, the cultural filters (or levels) are porous to the extent that its different components can interact and intermingle in a continuous, synergetic way. This is a participatory process in which members of the society have access at any given moment to its different economic, social or religious strata. The wake serves as a school of love, and the men who want to attract women, display their skill by grinding huge quantities of coffee beans. More than to these potential suitors, however, benefit accrues to the coffee owners "who have waited many days for an opportunity to have a dead person and an optimist resolve the thorniest and most difficult problems of their industry" (151). This example demonstrates how a certain economic problem (grinding coffee) is resolved within the socioeconomic system of La Sierpe.

This society generates and sustains certain customs and values in accordance with the needs of its members. The practice of weeping for the deceased is "one of the activities on the Atlantic coast which offers the most curious and extravagant variations" (151), and the reader enters the domain of folklore. The queen of the professional weepers is Pacha Pérez, who, like La Marquesita, "was swallowed up by legend" (151). Like many of García Márquez's characters, she undergoes a process of exaggeration, and she was "a skinny and authoritarian woman who, it is said, was changed into a snake by the devil at the age of 185" (151). She had "the hallucinating and satanic ability to compress the whole life story of a dead person into a single wailing" (151). The narrator draws his information from the oral tradition of the "street voice," the anonymous multitude of voices which have transformed Pacha Pérez.

Another figure created by this oral tradition is Pánfilo who has attended all the wakes for the last 30 years. What distinguishes Pánfilo from all the other prayer reciters is that "the rosary that he says, and its mysteries and its oration, are composed by him through the original, complicated use of Catholic literature and the superstitions of the Sierpe" (152). Pacha Pérez and Pánfilo not only represent popular creations of the folklore of La Sierpe, but they also interfuse the traditional values of Catholicism and the indigenous beliefs of La Sierpe. Pánfilo, like his predecessors, "has also melted into legend" (153). Power in this society is not permanent, whether it is acquired through heredity or skill, and its very permutability and transitoriness underline the fragility of all power. At some point, it will end because its form and exercise are indissolubly linked to its human agent. The danger is to let any one form of power become an agent of repression that reifies the human dimension and reduces it to an object. La Sierpe's internal self-regulating system converts power into a legendary expression which fits its fluid, permutable socioeconomic structure.

The Final Stage: Death in La Sierpe

The fourth chronicle, "The Happy Dead Man," offers a detailed account of how the inhabitants of La Sierpe bury their dead, and continues the marginalization of the dead man. La Sierpe's inhabitants show an apparently total lack of respect for the deceased, and the carpenter must quickly construct a coffin because "whoever needs the casket has been stretched out in a corner for at least six hours, rotting away among the pigs and chickens" (162). Besides the ironic treatment of traditional practices associated with death in which the serious and somber dominate, the reader soon discovers that physical death does not put an end to the relationship between life and death. The dead are normally buried in the cemetery located in La Guaripa without any need for formality or official control: "There they are, crammed together and unidentifiable, buried under a pile of crosses, those anonymous men, women and children, victims of malaria and dysentery. Or the swollen, deformed bodies of one out of every ten bitten by snakes" (162-63). In this space which seems to have lost its sacred aura and which can apparently be occupied by anyone, two kinds of deaths are excluded: "Only those who died by drowning or machete attacks are denied burial in the humid and narrow cemetery of La Guaripa" (163). The drowned person is excluded because "it is an unnatural death in the strange moral code of La Sierpe" (163). The word "strange" is not meant to be ironic, for many "marginal" societies possess "strange" beliefs, customs and rites concerning death when viewed from an ethnocentric perspective. García Márquez presents death as an internal component of this culture and it does not require further analysis as to its propriety or justification.

The boisterous ceremony which accompanies the return trip of the deceased, and during which he is further marginalized, reflects the fluidity and accessibility of a socioeconomic system in which the living and dead continue to communicate through the different porous filters of the society. Socially, the return trip gives rise to a continuous fiesta, and the trip is interrupted by numerous stops: "During one day and half a night, at least, the group splashes through the swamp, opening up new paths, drinking, talking, carrying a casket through whose joints the thick, foul smell of the dead person escapes" (163). This ceremony, which seems to belong to the realm of folklore and popular culture, differs from the fundamental cultural values of La Sierpe. The ceremony emphasizes physical participation to the point of suggesting a kind of "mindlessness": that is, mental participation is not necessary to give the ceremony meaning. Although some writers might consider popular culture unworthy of serious attention, García Márquez believes that it is a living entity which manifests itself in these apparently strange customs: "As I've already said, my grandmother's stories probably gave me the first clues. The myths, legends and beliefs of the people in her town were, in a very natural way, all part of her everyday life. With her in mind, I suddenly realized that I wasn't inventing anything at all but simply capturing and recounting a world of omens, premonitions, cures and superstitions that is authentically ours, truly Latin American. Remember those men in Colombia who get worms out of cow's ears by saying prayers, for example. Our day-to-day life in Latin America is full of this kind of thing."[28] Their double marginalization (they are part of a marginal society which performs its own marginalizing operations) has the effect of intensifying them and giving them a more universal quality.

Living (or popular) culture acts as an effective cultural filter through which the inhabitants can communicate. In the ceremony of the happy dead person, "the corpse informs those who are taking him to be buried if he agrees or is dissatisfied with his state" (164). When the cultural filters are closed, communication ceases and society starts to atrophy, fragment and finally disintegrate. In this ceremony, however, the cessation of life does not signal the end of communication. This continuous communication is symbolized by the song entitled "The Harvest of Deep Sorrow," which is sung "during the harvest and during the digging of graves" (164). The poem which concludes the series on La Sierpe has a "retrogressive relationship to the prose texts. The expression of a simplistic philosophy of possession/dispossession, like the fugacity to which it alludes, has a concrete sociocultural character to the extent that the whole text has it."[29] The fugacity which seems to characterize the human context of this society and its fragility are also warning signals of a more fundamental dilemma in Latin America.

La Sierpe already prefigures the future Macondo in terms of its marginality, isolation, and its self-determination and conspicuous lack of outside intervention. La Sierpe is a fragile society which has yet not been alienated from itself. In many ways, the history and literature of Latin America offer studies in alienation, heavily influenced by outside forces. Cultural monologism and hegemony have imposed silence on indigenous voices, and in these texts García Márquez has attempted to give these anonymous voices a precarious and diffuse presence. He realizes that, while he cannot overcome the centuries of voicelessness, it does lie within his grasp to set up a network of heterophonic dialogism. Although marginality of one type or another has characterized much of the historical evolution of the continent, there still remain places where this marginality can be transcended through an interior-exterior movement. La Sierpe, like that early Macondo, seems to stand on the threshold of innocence before it develops a historical conscience, and García Márquez is fully aware that its static position cannot last. La Sierpe is not a utopia, a projection of an idealistic sociocultural system, for García Márquez is not given to such facile formulations.   La Sierpe is strikingly devoid of internecine politics and any kind of historical materialism, and, in the final analysis, it stands as an example of a "marginal" society which may or may not assume the responsibility of developing its own sociohistorical conscience in relation to the outside world.

Notes

1.   This chapter was originally published in slightly different form in *Chasqui*, XVI.1 (February, 1987), 45-53.

2.   Gabriel García Márquez, *Obra periodística Vol. 2 Entre cachacos I*, ed. Jacques Gilard (Barcelona: Editorial Bruguera, 1982), 23. Translation is mine.

3.   Gabriel García Márquez, *Obra periodística Vol. 1 Textos costeños*, ed. Jacques Gilard (Barcelona: Bruguera, 1981), 867. Translation is mine. All ensuing quotes from this text will be given in parentheses with page numbers.

4.   In "Big Mama's Funeral," La Sierpe finds its place in the geography of the short story: "Now that the nation, which was shaken to its vitals, has recovered its balance: now that the bagpipers of San Jacinto, the smugglers of Guajira, the rice planters of Sinú, the prostitutes of Guacamayal, the wizards of La Sierpe, and the banana workers of Aracataca have folded up their tents to recover from the exhausting vigil and have regained their serenity..." Gabriel García Márquez, *Collected Stories* (New York: Harper & Row, 1984), 184.

5.   Gabriel García Márquez, *Entre cachacos I*, 117. Translation is mine. All ensuing quotes from the La Sierpe chronicles will come from this edition, and page numbers will be given in parentheses.

6.   The best known example is the opening sentence of *OHYS* which offers the reader a prolepsis which is actually suspended several times until this event rejoins the chronology of events later on in the novel: "Many years later, as he faced the firing squad, Colonel Aureliano Buendía was to remember that distant afternoon when his father took him to discover ice." Gabriel García Márquez, *One Hundred Years of Solitude*, trans. Gregory Rabassa (New York: Avon Books, 1971), 11.

7.   Oswald Ducrot and Tzvetan Todorov, *Encyclopedic Dictionary of the Sciences of Language*, trans. Catherine Anne Porter (Baltimore: The Johns Hopkins UP, 1983), 343.

8.   Ducrot, 343.

9.   Ducrot, 342.

10.   Ducrot, 360.

11.   Ducrot, 360.

12.   Wilfrido H. Corral, "La serie de La Sierpe: García Márquez y la disolución informativa," *Texto crítico*, 3.8 (September-December, 1977), 78. All translations are mine.

13.   Corral, 74-5.

14.   Jonathan Culler, *Structuralist Poetics: Structuralism, Linguistics and the Study of Literature* (Ithaca: Cornell UP, 1976), 137.

15.   Culler, 137.

16.   Tzvetan Todorov, *Mikhail Bakhtin: The Dialogical Principle*, trans. Wlad Godzich (Minneapolis: The Univ. of Minnesota Press, 1984), 71.

17.   Todorov, *The Dialogical Principle*, 73.

18.   Virgilio López Lemus, *García Márquez: Una vocación incontenible* (Habana: Editorial Letras Cubanas, 1982), 90. Translation is mine. One of the symbolic examples to which the author refers is the socialist vision of equality in Macondo's early stages: "José Arcadio Buendía, who was the most enterprising man ever to be seen in the village, had set up the placement of the houses in such a way that from all of them one could reach the river and draw water with the same effort, and he had lined up the streets with such good sense that no house got more sun than another during the hot time of the day" Gabriel García Márquez, *One Hundred Years of Solitude*, trans. Gregory Rabassa (New York: Avon Books, 1971), 18. In addition, Colonel Aureliano Buendía and Fernanda del Carpio embody the bankrupt policies and ideas of the Liberal and Conservative parties, both of which García Márquez rejects. After the Biblical deluge, which traditionally symbolizes renewal and rebirth, the Buendías continue along the same path, refusing to change and start anew.

19.   Octavio Paz captures this idea in his Nobel Prize lecture: "Reflecting on the now does not mean relinquishing the future or forgetting the past. The present is the meeting place for the two directions of time. It should not be confused with facile hedonism. What do we know about the present? Nothing or almost nothing. Yet the poets do know one thing: the present is the source of presences. The intact present, recently unearthed, shakes off the dust of centuries, smiles, and suddenly takes wing and flies out through the window. A simultaneous plurality of time and presence: modernity breaks with the immediate past only to recover an age-old past. Then the door of perception opens slightly and the *other time* appears, the real time we had been seeking without knowing it: the present, the presence," *In Search of the Present*, trans. Anthony Stanton (New York: Harcourt Brace Jovanovich, 1990), 32, 33 and 34.

20.   Gabriel García Márquez, *One Hundred Years of Solitude*, 59.

21. Corral, "La serie de La Sierpe," 76.

22. Ducrot, *Encyclopedic Dictionary*, 278.

23. Corral, 81.

24. Richard Schacht, *Alienation* (New York: Anchor Books, 1970), 93.

25. Corral, 81.

26. Corral, 84.

27. Corral, 83-84.

28. Gabriel García Márquez and Plinio Apuleyo Mendoza, *The Fragrance of Guava*, trans. Ann Wright (London: Verso Editions, 1983), 59.

29. Corral, 87.

Conclusion

García Márquez, Bigeneric Writing and the Open Work

If one clear conclusion emerges from this study, it is that the minor works must be studied to be able to understand the major ones. The journalistic pieces represent "minor works" primarily because critics have preferred to relegate them to the status of inconsequential pre-texts within García Márquez's total production. Moreover, critics have refused to consider his work as an expression of his bigeneric writing. García Márquez flatly rejects this idea: "I don't think there is any difference. The sources are the same, the material is the same, the resources and the language are the same. *The Journal of the Plague Year* by Daniel Defoe is a great novel and [John Hersey's] *Hiroshima* is a great work of journalism. In journalism just one fact that is false prejudices the entire work. In contrast, in fiction one single fact that is true gives legitimacy to the entire work. That's the only difference and it lies in the commitment of the writer. A novelist can do anything he wants so long as he makes people believe in it."[1] The majority of critical studies gloss over García Márquez's journalistic writings in their rush to focus on his "major works" and confine their comments on his journalism to the techniques which contribute to his fiction writing. While critics have maintained a strict division between García Márquez the novelist and journalist, the author has repeatedly underscored the bigeneric nature of his writing: "The writer's very attempt to portray reality often leads him to a distorted view of it. In trying to transpose reality he can end up losing contact with it, in an ivory tower, as they say. Journalism is a very good guard against that. That's why I have always tried to keep on doing journalism because it keeps me in contact with the real world, particularly political journalism and politics."[2] This study has focused only on García Márquez's journalism from 1948 to 1955 because it is during this pivotal period that he developed the macroelements that would lay the foundations for his subsequent writing.

In this context the columns, articles and feature stories of García Márquez represent the massive part of the Hemingway iceberg which has remained submerged until recently: "Hemingway said that the literary work is like the iceberg: the huge, floating mass that we see proves invulnerable because underwater it is supported by the other seven-eights of its volume."[3] As Pedro Sorela explains:

> García Márquez's journalism, and above all its continued success at different times and in different countries, is in itself an effective antidote to the more antiquated academic and professional theories which attempt to fit journalism into neat, well-defined categories, as if the history of communication were a kind of geometry. The 4,500 pages in question represent the irrefutable proof that, while safeguarding the basic principle of truth and two or three others, journalism encompasses or must encompass everything, that every subject and scenario require journalistic treatment, that the best education for the journalist is that which develops his capacity to know how to choose the most appropriate form at any given moment. And all that is necessary so that the reader, in that case, gets the story with the greatest degree of clarity, reliability and pleasure. That is what it is all about.[4]

The visible part of the iceberg has always been García Márquez's literary work, but recently, and especially since the publication in 1981-82 of his journalistic writing from 1948 to 1960, the situation has started to change. The seven-eights of the iceberg to which García Márquez refers, contain the journalistic writings, and now the weight of its enormous quantity and quality is beginning to emerge.

It would be a mistake to limit the study of García Márquez's journalism to a small number of texts without recognizing that each note, column, article or feature story make up part of a single Text which García Márquez started to write with his first journalistic piece. Indeed, a writer only writes one Text composed of different books, and the Garciamarquian Text includes his journalism. The Text of García Márquez is the product of bigeneric writing, and this study has exposed and examined the hidden mass of the iceberg which not only supports but lays the foundations of all his subsequent work.

The Garciamarquian Text is also an Infinite Text which reflects the constant interplay between hypotexts and hypertexts. García Márquez's hypotexts are personal, cultural and literary. The most prominent ones are the Coast, the costeños, mamagallismo, the Group of Barranquilla, Kafka, Hemingway and Faulkner. If personal and external hypotexts pervade his journalistic pieces, his first short stories are dominated by external ones. In his journalism García Márquez succeeds in overcoming and/or integrating the outside hypotexts by filtering them through his personal experience which is deeply rooted in costeño culture. These external hypotexts, which dominate his first stories, collide with his personal and cultural hypotexts in his journalism. García Márquez subjects Kafka to the permanent sense of humor of costeño mamagallismo and writes a jirafa entitled "Caricature of Kafka." If García Márquez abandons Kafka during the first phase of his journalism, the hypotexts of Faulkner and, to a lesser degree, of Hemingway, continue to expand and hypertextualize with his work.

The continuous hypo-hypertextual interaction in his journalism liberates and energizes this writing which does not distinguish between genres:

> Because the heterodoxy of García Márquez is practiced in nearly all the "genres" of journalism, and that is what matters and not the 4,500 pages: the daily column, the editorial and anonymous news item, the film criticism, the news report, the foreign news story, the feature story, the nonfiction novel, the unusual news story. No doubt he is stronger in some areas (the feature story) than others (his film criticism), but

>in any case he does it with an unmistakable personal style, which not only raises him above the multitudinous limbo of journalistic writing, but also inspires considerable optimism in those who believe in the permanent renewal of genres as the indispensable requirement for the survival of print journalism.[5]

García Márquez's writing mocks criticism and genres, and his works offer a space where the genres crisscross, collide, combine and separate continuously to create an Infinite Text that is never finalized, where the word recovers its human heterophony. Unlike the traditional conception of the journalist, García Márquez, similar to the polyphonist Dostoevsky, perceives "in the struggle of opinions and ideologies (of various epochs) an incomplete dialogue on ultimate questions."[6] In García Márquez's bigeneric writing "the word of the journalist, when introduced into the polyphonic novel, submits to unfinalized and infinite dialogue."[7] The Infinite Text of García Márquez is a constantly open(ing) work, an interactive process between journalism and literature.

Alejo Carpentier, during a session on journalism, concluded by affirming that "the journalist invigorates the great novel of the future."[8] Carpentier's words clearly point the way for studying and understanding the work of García Márquez. The *authentic* work of García Márquez originated in the journalistic pieces that he wrote between 1948 and 1955, and journalism has continued to energize and strengthen the great novel that he is writing. As Rodríguez Núñez rightly observes, "the journalistic work is not, when it is carried out with aesthetic and human dignity, and with full awareness of its possibilities, an ancillary, secondary aspect in the process of literary creation."[9] Beyond representing the primary source of the Infinite Text of García Márquez, journalism continues to be "the noblest profession in the world," and the Nobel Prize for Literature which the Swedish Academy awarded him in 1982, is also a Nobel Prize for Journalism. The work of García Márquez surpasses the generic frontiers to enter into the incomplete and vital dialogue of human heteroglossia, and his bigeneric writing continues to recover and revitalize a multitude of voices. The work of García Márquez enters fully into the dialogical world of Bakhtin where "there is neither a first nor a last word and there are no limits to the dialogical context."[10]

Notes

1.   George Plimpton, ed., *The Writer's Chapbook: A Compendium of Fact, Wit, and Advice from the 20th Century's Preeminent Writers* (New York: Viking Penguin, 1989), 257.

2.   George Plimpton, *The Writer's Chapbook*, 257.

3.   Mario Vargas Llosa, *García Márquez: Historia de un deicidio* (Barcelona: Barral, 1971), 150. Translation is mine.

4.   Pedro Sorela, *El otro García Márquez: Los años difíciles* (Madrid: Mondadori, 1988), 275. All translations are mine.

5.   Pedro Sorela, 275.

6.   M. M. Bakhtin, *Speech Genres and Other Late Essays*, trans. Vern W. McGee (Austin: Univ. of Texas Press, 1986), 151.

7.   M. M. Bakhtin, 152.

8.   Quoted in: Víctor Rodríguez Núñez, "La peregrinación de la jirafa: García Márquez, su periodismo costeño," *Casa de la Américas* 23.137 (March-April, 1983), 39. Translations are mine.

9.   Rodríguez Núñez, 39.

10.   M. M. Bakhtin, 170.

Bibliography

Ayala Poveda, Fernando. *Manual de literatura colombiana*. Bogotá: Educar Editores, 1986.

Bakhtin, M. M. *The Dialogic Imagination: Four Essays*. Trans. Caryl Emerson and Michael Holquist. Austin: University of Texas Press, 1981.

Bakhtin, M. M. *Problems of Dostoevsky's Poetics*. Trans. Caryl Emerson. Minneapolis: University of Minnesota Press, 1985.

Bakhtin, M. M. *Speech Genres and Other Late Essays*. Trans. Vern M.McGee. Ed. Caryl Emerson and Michael Holquist. Austin: University of Texas Press, 1986.

Bal, Mieke. *Narratology: Introduction to the Theory of Narrative*. Trans. Christine van Boheemen. Toronto: University of Toronto Press, 1985.

Barthes, Roland. *Critical Essays*. Trans. Richard Howard. Evanston: Northwestern UP, 1972.

Barthes, Roland. *S/Z*. Trans. Richard Howard. New York: Hill and Wang, 1974.

Boncenne, Pierre. "Gabriel García Márquez s'explique." *Lire* 51 (November, 1979), 49-68.

Brushwood, John S. *The Spanish American Novel: A Twentieth-Century Survey*. Austin: University of Texas Press, 1975.

Carpentier, Alejo. *Tientos y diferencias*. Buenos Aires: Calicanto Editorial, 1976.

Cohan, Steve and Linda M. Shires. *Telling Stories: A Theoretical Analysis of Narration*. London: Routledge, 1988.

Corral, Wilfrido H. "La serie de la Sierpe: García Márquez y la disolución informativa." *Texto crítico* 3.8 (September-December, I977), 73-87.

Culler, Jonathan. *Structuralist Poetics, Structuralism, Linguistics and the Study of Literature*. Ithaca: Cornell UP, 1976.

Dällenbach, Lucien. "Intertexte et autotexte." *Poétique* 27 (1976), 282-96.

Ducrot, Oswald and Tzvetan Todorov. *Encyclopedic Dictionary of the Sciences of Language*. Trans. Catherine Porter. Baltimore: The Johns Hopkins UP, I983.

Fenton, Charles A. *The Apprenticeship of Ernest Hemingway: The Early Years*. New York: Viking, I968.

Fishkin, Shelley Fisher. *From Fact to Fiction: Journalism & Imaginative Writing in America*. Oxford: Oxford UP, 1985.

Fonnegra, Gabriel. *La prensa en Colombia*. Bogotá: El Ancora Editores, 1984.

García Márquez, Gabriel. *Collected Stories*. New York: Harper & Row, I984.

García Márquez, Gabriel. *The Autumn of the Patriarch*. Trans. Gregory Rabassa. New York: Avon Books, I977.

García Márquez, Gabriel. *De viaje por los países socialistas: 90 días en la "cortina de hierro"*. Bogotá: La Oveja Negra, I986.

García Márquez, Gabriel. *El general en su laberinto*. Bogotá: La Oveja Negra, 1989.

García Márquez, Gabriel. *La soledad de América Latina*. Cali: Corporación Editorial Universitaria de Colombia, 1982.

García Márquez, Gabriel. *Obra periodística, Vol. I: Textos costeños.*Ed. Jacques Gilard. Barcelona: Bruguera, 1981.

García Márquez, Gabriel. *Obra periodística, Vol. 2: Entre cachacos I.* Ed. Jacques Gilard. Barcelona: Bruguera, 1982.

García Márquez, Gabriel. *Obra periodística, Vol. 3: Entre cachacos II.* Ed. Jacques Gilard. Barcelona: Bruguera, 1982.

García Márquez, Gabriel. *Obra periodística, Vol. 4: De Europa a América.* Ed. Jacques Gilard. Barcelona: Bruguera, 1983.

García Márquez, Gabriel. *One Hundred Years of Solitude.* Trans. Gregory Rabassa. New York: Avon Books, 1971.

García Márquez, Gabriel and Plinio Apuleyo Mendoza. *The Fragrance of Guava.* Trans. Ann Wright. London: Verso Editions, 1983.

García Márquez, Gabriel. *The Story of a Shipwrecked Sailor.* Trans. Randolph Hogan. New York: Vintage Books, 1987.

Genette, Gérard. *Narrative Discourse: An Essay in Method.* Trans. Jane E. Levin. Ithaca: Cornell UP, 1983.

Genette, Gérard. *Narrative Discourse Revisited.* Trans. Jane E. Lewin. Ithaca: Cornell UP, 1988.

Genette, Gérard. *Palimpsestes: La Littérature au Second Degré.* Paris: Editions du Seuil, 1982.

Gilard, Jacques. "García Márquez en 1950 et 1951: quelques données sur la genèse d'une oeuvre." *Caravelle: Cahiers du Monde Hispanique et Luso-brésilien* 26 (1976), 123-46.

Gilard, Jacques. "La obra periodística de García Márquez, 1954-1956." *Revista de crítica literaria latinoamericana* (Lima) 2.4 (July/December, 1976), 151-76.

González, Anibal. "The Ends of the Text: Journalism in the Fiction of Gabriel García Márquez." In: Julio Orega, ed. *Gabriel García Márquez and the Powers of Fiction*. Austin: University of Texas Press, 1988, 62-73.

González Echevarría, Roberto. *Alejo Carpentier: The Pilgrim at Home*. Ithaca: Cornell UP, 1977.

Harss, Luis and Barbara Dohman. *Into the Mainstream: Conversations with Latin-American Writers*. New York: Harper & Row, 1969.

Hayes, Aden. "Hemingway y García Márquez: Tarde o temprano." In: *Violencia y literatura en Colombia*.   Ed. Jonathan Tittler. Madrid: Orígenes, 1989, 53-62.

Hemingway, Ernest. *Death in the Afternoon*. New York: Charles Scribner's Sons, I960.

Holquist, Michael. *Dialogism: Bakhtin and his World*. London: Routledge, 1990.

Iser, Wolfgang. *The Act of Reading: A Theory of Aesthetic Response*. Baltimore: The Johns Hopkins UP, I980.

Lévi-Strauss, Claude. *The Savage Mind*. Chicago: University of Chicago Press, 1970.

López de Martinez, Adelaida. Review of *Chronicle of a Death Foretold* by Gabriel García Márquez. *Chasqui* X.2-3 (February-May, I98I), 70-2.

López de Suazo Algar, Antonio. *Diccionario del periodismo*. Madrid: Ediciones Pirámide, 1985.

López Lemus, Virgilio. *García Márquez: Una vocación incontenible*. Habana: Editorial Letras Cubanas, I982.

Márquez Rodríguez, Alexis. *La comunicación impresa: Teoría y práctica del lenguaje periodístico*. Caracas: Ediciones Centauro, l976.

Minta, Stephen. *García Márquez: Writer of Colombia*. New York: Harper & Row, l987.

Morin, Violette. *El tratamiento periodístico de la información*. Trans. Alfonso Espinet. Barcelona: Mouton and Co. and ATE, 1974.

Morson, Gary Saul and Caryl Emerson, ed. *Rethinking Bakhtin: Extensions and Challenges*. Evanston: Nortwestern UP, 1989.

Ong, Walter J. *Orality and Literacy: The Technologizing of the Word*. New York: Methuen, 1983.

Pineda Botero, Alvaro. *Teoría de la novela*. Bogotá: Plaza y Janés, 1987.

Plimpton, George, ed. *The Writer's Chapbook: A Compendium of Fact, Wit and Advice from the 20th Century's Preeminent Writers*. New York: Penquin, 1989.

Prada Oropeza, Renato. *El lenguaje narrativo: Prolegómenos para una semiótica narrativa*. Costa Rica: Editorial Universitaria Centroamericana, 1979.

Pratt, Mary Louise. *Toward a Speech Act Theory of Literary Discourse*. Bloomington: Indiana UP, l977.

Prince, Gerald. *Dictionary of Narratology*. Lincoln: University of Nebraska Press, 1989.

Rabell, Carmen. *Periodismo y ficción en Crónica de una muerte anuniciada*. Santiago: Instituto Profesional del Pacífico, l985.

Rentería Mantilla, Alfonso. *García Márquez habla de García Márquez*. Bogotá: Rentería Editores, I979.

Rivadeneira Prada, Raúl. *La opinión pública: Análisis, estructura y métodos para su estudio*. México: Editorial Trillas, 1976.

Rivadeneira Prada, Raúl. *Periodismo: La teoría general de los sistemas y la ciencia de la comunicación*. México: Editorial Trillas, 1983.

Rodríguez Núñez, Victor. "La peregrinación de la jirafa. García Márquez: su periodismo costeño." *Casa de las Américas* 23.137 (March/ April, I983), 27-39.

Schacht, Richard. *Alienation*. New York: Anchor Books, I970.

Sorela, Pedro. *El otro García Márquez: Los años difíciles*. Madrid: Mondadori, 1988.

Spengler, Oswald. *The Decline of the West*. 2 Vols. Trans. Charles Francis Atkinson. New York: Knopf, I983.

Todorov, Tzvetan. *Mikhail Bakhtin: The Dialogical Principle*. Trans. Wlad Godzich. Minneapolis: University of Minnesota Press, I984.

Vargas, Germán. *Sobre literatura colombiana*. Bogotá: Fundación Simón y Lola Guberek, 1985.

Vargas Llosa, Mario. *García Márquez: Historia de un deicidio*. Barcelona: Barral Editores, I97I.

Vargas Llosa, Mario. *The Storyteller*. Trans. Helen Lane. New York: Farrar, Straus and Giroux, 1989.

Weber, Ronald. *The Literature of Fact: Literary Nonfcition in American Writing*. Athens: Ohio UP, 1985.

Webster's II New Riverside Dictionary. Boston: Houghton Mifflin, 1984.

Weiner, Richard. *Webster's New World Dictionary of Media and Communications*. New York: Simon & Schuster, 1990.

Williams, Raymond L. *Gabriel García Márquez*. Boston: Twayne, 1985.

Wolfe, Tom and E. W. Johnson, eds. *The New Juornalism (With an Anthology)*. New York: Harper & Row, 1973.

Name Index

Footnote numbers will appear in italics.

Thematic Index

About the Author

Robert L. Sims is currently an Associate Professor of Foreign Languages at Virginia Commonwealth University in Richmond, Virginia. He received his B.A. in French from the University of Michigan (1966) and his M.A. and Ph.D. from the University of Wisconsin-Madison (1968, 1973). He served as a Peace Corps Volunteer in Colombia, South America from 1968 to 1970. Professor Sims has published widely in the fields of twentieth-century French and Latin American literature. His publications include many articles which have appeared in *Chasqui, Hispania, Nottingham French Studies, Revista Iberoamericana, Revista de Estudios Colombianos* and *Hispanic Journal.* He has also published two books on García Márquez: *The Evolution of Myth in Gabriel García Márquez from La hojarasca to Cien años de soledad* (Miami: Ediciones Universal, 1982) and *El primer García Márquez: Un estudio de su periodismo de 1948 a 1955* (Potomac, Maryland: Scripta Humanistica, 1991).